BOB BUNN • GENERAL EDITOR

Path of PURITY

A FAMILY GUIDE

LifeWay Press®
Nashville, Tennessee

ISBN: 978-1-4158-6876-8

Item Number: 005271289

Dewey Decimal Classification Number: 649

Subject Heading: SEXUAL ABSTINENCE \ PARENT AND CHILD \ CHILD REARING

Printed in the United States of America

Student Ministry Publishing

LifeWay Church Resources

One Lifeway Plaza

Nashville, TN 37234-0174

We believe the Bible has God for its author; salvation for its end;
and truth, without any mixture of error, for its matter and that all Scripture is totally true
and trustworthy. The 2000 statement of *The Baptist Faith and Message*
is our doctrinal guideline.

Table of
CONTENTS

About the CONTRIBUTORS

◆ **BOB BUNN** serves as an editor in the Student Ministry Publishing area of LifeWay Christian Resources. He oversees the production of *Living with Teenagers* magazine. Bob also works on the True Love Waits planning team and was the general editor for *Path of Purity*. He contributed chapter 4, "Parents and the Path of Purity."

◆ **PAM GIBBS** is the girls ministry specialist at LifeWay Christian Resources. In addition to working on a wide variety of girls resources and leading conferences for girls and parents, Pam serves on the True Love Waits planning team. She contributed the markers for younger and older youth and for singleness and engagement. She also wrote the detours for abuse, homosexuality, and living together.

◆ **JIMMY HESTER** serves as the senior director of Student Ministry Publishing at LifeWay Christian Resources. As a co-founder of True Love Waits, he has been with the movement since its inception. He currently facilitates the TLW planning team and contributed chapter 1, "An Introduction to True Love Waits," and chapter 3, "TLW 3.0: A Path of Purity."

◆ **JEFF LAND** is an editorial project leader in the Childhood Ministry Publishing area of LifeWay Christian Resources. Jeff wrote the markers for childhood.

◆ **RICHARD ROSS** serves as a professor of student ministry at Southwestern Theological Seminary in Fort Worth, Texas. He has written several books related to student ministry, including his most recent work, *Student Ministry and the Supremacy of Christ* (CrossBooks, 2009). Richard is a co-founder of True Love Waits and wrote the material for chapter 2, "The Current State of the Abstinence Movement."

◆ **PAUL TURNER** is the lead student ministry specialist at LifeWay Christian Resources. Paul encourages student ministry leaders throughout the country and around the world. He serves on the True Love Waits planning team and wrote chapter 10, "The Parent Partnership."

◆ **MIKE WAKEFIELD** is an editorial project leader in the Student Ministry Publishing area of LifeWay Christian Resources. He coordinates several dated and undated resources—including resources related to True Love Waits through the TLW planning team. Mike wrote the markers for younger youth, older youth, and for college and marriage. He also contributed the detours for sexual activity, pregnancy/abortion, and pornography.

◆ **EMILY COLE** served as the production editor for *Path of Purity*. She works in Student Ministry Publishing at LifeWay and has helped shaped numerous resources, including *ec*, a monthly devotion magazine for teens, and all girls' ministry products.

◆ **AMY LYON** served as the graphic designer for *Path of Purity*. Amy contributes to a wide array of student-related resources in the Student Ministry Publishing area of LifeWay Christian Resources.

AN INTRODUCTION
TO TRUE LOVE WAITS

BY JIMMY HESTER

I n the early 1990s, teenagers were bombarded with
sexual messages from advertisers, television producers,
moviemakers, fashion designers, and media channels of every
form. This led to a common belief that everyone was having sex,
especially their peers and young adults. At the same time, adults
bought into the same notion and told teenagers, "We know you're
sexually active, so here are condoms to protect you from disease
and unwanted pregnancy."

Out of this culture came the cry from godly teenagers
(supported by their parents): "No! We're not all sexually active, and
we don't think it's right to have sex until you're married!"

So in the fall of 1992, Richard Ross and I sat in the cafeteria
of the Baptist Sunday School Board (now LifeWay Christian
Resources) and outlined on a napkin what has come to be known
as True Love Waits. And for nearly two decades now, we have
witnessed God's work among teenagers who have been willing to
model God's plan that reserves sexual activity for marriage.

True Love Waits

True Love Waits (TLW) is an international campaign challenging and empowering students to make a commitment to sexual purity, live it every day, and proclaim it to others. At its core, True Love Waits is about following God's plan for purity.

Most students discover True Love Waits through their church or student organization. Many churches hold study groups, worship services, and special events focused on purity. Student organizations in schools and communities carry the message through their regular programming. But no matter how a student gets involved, the challenge of True Love Waits is to make and keep this commitment:

> *Believing that true love waits, I make a commitment to God, myself, my family, my friends, my future mate, and my future children to a lifetime of purity including sexual abstinence from this day until the day I enter a biblical marriage relationship.*

Since True Love Waits was officially launched in 1993, millions of students all over the world have signed commitment cards and displayed them in public places to express their beliefs about purity. Lives have been saved and families have been spared the consequences of premature sexual activity. Cultures have been changed—all because students were willing to take a stand for purity.

Fresh Approaches

The advancement of True Love Waits has been interesting. The first two years were devoted to establishing the movement within the teenage culture. This was primarily accomplished through church youth groups. But other student organizations began expressing interest, and they soon joined the True Love Waits campaign's efforts.

- ◆ **June 1994:** 102,000 cards displayed at the Southern Baptist Convention, Orlando, Florida
- ◆ **July 1994:** 210,000 cards displayed on The Mall in front of The Capitol, Washington, D.C.
- ◆ **August 1995:** 220,000 cards displayed at the Baptist World Alliance, Buenos Aires, Argentina

In 1995, teenagers spoke again. They said, "It is great that we can be part of True Love Waits in our churches, but we have friends at school who need to hear this message." So along came *True Love Waits Goes Campus*. The initial focus of taking the message to secondary school and college campuses continues today, even though the official theme is rarely used.

+ **February 1996:** 340,000 cards stacked "Thru the Roof" at the Georgia Dome, Atlanta, Georgia

True Love Waits Goes Campus was launched at the Thru the Roof event in Atlanta in February 1996. The plan was to work toward an annual event on campuses around Valentine's Day each year. Activities happen throughout the year, but February has become the time when many True Love Waits events and promotions take place.

On Valentine's Day 1997, *True Love Waits Goes Campus* was conducted on secondary and college campuses. More than 500,000 commitment cards were distributed by LifeWay, but many church and school groups prepared their own cards. Local media coverage was extensive as students once again demonstrated their commitment to sexual purity.

True Love Waits Goes Campus took a different twist in 1998. On Valentine's Day, youth groups collected the names of students making commitments and sent them to state TLW leaders. Each leader compiled a list of names for his state and presented it to his governor and other state officials. The state leaders also submitted their lists to the True Love Waits team in Nashville, Tennessee. In April 1998, these reports were taken to Washington, D.C., and personally delivered to the Surgeon General of the United States, and to several senators and representatives. A report was also included in the Congressional Record.

+ **October 1999:** 100,000 cards crossed the Golden Gate Bridge, San Francisco, California

As the new millennium approached, the True Love Waits team wanted to challenge teenagers to enter the future with a commitment to purity. The team developed the theme *Crossing Bridges with Purity*, which was launched on Valentine's Day 1999. Churches and student organizations carried commitment cards over local bridges to symbolize their commitment to purity. The cards eventually ended up in San Francisco where they were carried across the Golden Gate Bridge on October 2, 1999, by 1,500 teenagers.

On December 31, 1999, two hours before Millennium Island welcomed the year 2000, a group in Australia prayed for the cards that crossed the Golden Gate Bridge.

- **February 2001:** 31,338 online pledges through *Seize the Net*
- **February 2002:** 82,000 online pledges through *Seize the Net Goes Live*

Following *Crossing Bridges with Purity*, the TLW team focused on a part of culture that would be inviting to teenagers and provide a unique way to gather and display commitments. On Valentine's Day 2001, *True Love Waits: Seize the Net* took place. Teenagers were invited to register their commitments to purity at a website which kept a running total of online pledges—from the beginning of Valentine's Day in Australia until it ended in Alaska. The theme was continued in 2002. To give greater life to the focus, *Seize the Net Goes Live*, a live event originating in Ft. Worth, Texas, was held on Valentine's eve and was relayed via satellite to local churches and student groups across the United States.

In 2003, True Love Waits returned to its roots—the home. *True Love Waits Goes Home* carried a double meaning. First, it called teenagers and their families to make a commitment to purity (for the teenager, sexual purity until marriage; for parents, sexual purity within marriage). Second, it allowed everyone to remember the journey.

- **August 2004:** 450,000 cards on display in Athens, Greece during the Summer Olympics

True Love Waits celebrated the 10th anniversary of the first national display in 2004 with a rally and card display at The Parthenon in Nashville. Those cards were combined with cards from around the world to create an international display during the Summer Olympics in Athens, Greece, on August 22, 2004.

The True Blessing

Commitment card displays are always impressive, but the true blessing of True Love Waits is found in the testimonies of teenagers. It began at Youth Ministry National Conference 4 in 1993, when students from Tulip Grove Baptist Church in Old Hickory, Tennessee, testified about their True Love Waits commitments before the youth leaders in attendance, and it has continued to this day. From teenagers saying they made a commitment to purity long before they heard about True Love Waits to non-Christian teenagers making commitments to Christ as part of their commitment to purity to sexually-active teenagers who want their lives to be different now that they know about the importance of sexual purity, God continues to use True Love Waits for His purposes.

THE CURRENT STATE OF THE ABSTINENCE MOVEMENT

BY RICHARD ROSS

God calls believers to tell each other about His mighty works. Recounting what He has done brings glory to God and strengthens the faith of His children. In our day, God birthed, expanded, and now guides the True Love Waits movement. Recounting what He is doing makes perfect sense.

Positive Statistics

No one knows exactly how many students around the world have taken the True Love Waits pledge, but it is safe to say that millions of teenagers in the U.S.—and worldwide—have made the promise. And the results have been encouraging. Except for a blip from 2005 to 2007 (to be discussed later), the rates of teenage sexual activity and teen birth rates have been falling steadily since the early 1990s.[1]

As in *It's a Wonderful Life*, it is moving to consider all the tragedies that never have happened because of purity promises:

- ◆ Parents' hearts that never were broken;
- ◆ Teenagers who never contracted diseases;

* Dreams that never were shattered;
* Babies who weren't born into incomplete homes; and
* Believers who never felt estranged from God because of guilt.

Joyful Weddings

We often receive reports about weddings that unite two people who earlier had made True Love Waits promises. It now is common for them to alter their vows to include statements about that commitment to purity. In some instances, they ask the minister to say a few words about their pledges and lead them as they present True Love Waits rings to each other as a symbol of their commitment to each other and to building a legacy that will touch the next generation.[2]

While some students stumble, thousands of others make—and keep—purity promises and move into biblical marriages. They find deep joy in committed sexual relationships without flashbacks, emotional scarring, or guilt. By waiting until marriage, they experience the greatest delight in sex—just as God planned.

Broader Abstinence Movement

Careful observers credit True Love Waits with fostering much of the broader abstinence movement. When TLW came on the scene in 1993, the term "abstinence" was not commonly used. But as of 2010, a Google™ search produced millions of links. In addition, the Family Research Council has counted 1,000 abstinence programs around the U.S.[3]

Currently, more than 100 denominations and organizations are registered as official cooperating organizations with TLW. Most of them have committed incredible energy and resources toward placing the message of purity before teenagers, families, and churches. From the halls of Congress to youth room walls in churches, abstinence and purity are now very much a part of the national conversation about teenage sexuality.

Parents and Purity

In the early days of TLW, parents often sat on the sidelines as church leaders took the lead. Today, leaders are waking up to the fact that parents have the greatest potential to shape their children's purity decisions.

Parents' spiritual leadership in the home always has been God's ideal. His primary plan for getting truth into the lives of teenagers is to have them learn at the feet of their parents. While this truth will be covered more thoroughly in chapter 4, the role of parents is worth touching on now as we consider the current state of purity.

Research from the National Survey of Youth and Religion clearly indicates that parents are the single most important influence on the religious and spiritual lives of adolescents. Grandparents, other relatives, mentors, and youth workers can be very influential, but not more than parents.[4] Wise parents embrace the role of guiding their children toward purity, and wise church leaders will do all they can to equip parents for this valuable role.

Cause for Concern

Before the rise of TLW, teenage sexual activity increased for 20 consecutive years. Consequently, teen pregnancies, abortions, births, and sexually transmitted diseases also rose. Then, as noted, each of these statistics started to fall as True Love Waits began growing.

But a report from the Centers for Disease Control and Prevention noted that the declines had been stymied—and possibly reversed—in 2006 and 2007. Sexual activity, teen births, and sexual diseases all increased.[5]

In the years immediately following 1993, youth leaders, parents, and students leaned hard into the purity movement, and God received glory. But at some point, many youth leaders moved away from an annual focus on purity promises.

Thankfully, the numbers resumed their downward trend between 2007 and 2008, making the two previous years as a blip on the radar.[6] But the rise of 2005 through 2007 should be a wake-up call. Parents and church leaders can't let their guard down as they teach coming generations about living in purity.

Much Remains to Be Done

Believers can rejoice over victories, but much remains to be done. One Heritage Foundation study reported that 2.6 million teens become sexually active each year—about 7,000 a day. Around half of all high schoolers said they had been sexually active in the past, while one-third are currently active.[7]

Our current moral climate reflects a people who have turned from God. But we have hope. Some of God's greatest movements have erupted during times of spiritual darkness.

God wants parents and leaders to encourage purity among teenagers. But the spiritual preparation has to transcend that single issue. In their book, *Firefall: How God Has Shaped History Through Revivals*, Malcolm McDow and Alvin Reid wrote, "Ethical restructuring as a primary focus leads to short-lived changes... If we are to see an awakening in our day, let the revival for which we pray be a revival of holiness—a revival marked by an awesome respect for a sovereign God, brokenness over individual sin, and a passion for obedience."[8]

A Focus Every Year

Almost every Sunday morning, I'm in a different church, and I often hear things like, "Richard, we're thrilled with what God has done through True Love Waits—it's a powerful movement. In fact, we so believe in True Love Waits that we had a beautiful promise ceremony here three years ago."

I keep a smile on my face, but thoughts whirl through my mind: *Three years ago? Teens who entered puberty at 11 or 12 reach ninth grade with no chance to make a promise of purity? Middle school students bombarded with sexual messages go a year with no purity emphasis? Upperclassmen graduate with no chance to stand tall for purity in a worship celebration? Families with teenagers who join the church have to wait for years before they are challenged to slip a True Love Waits ring on their teens' fingers?*

Leaders might shy away from an annual ceremony because they don't want to ask a student to make so many promises while young, but they've missed the point. Teenagers don't need to make multiple promises. The annual invitation to participate in a ceremony should only be made:

1. To middle schoolers entering the student ministry.
2. To students who have committed their lives to Christ in the last year.
3. To students who have joined the church and have no TLW background.

Students who have made promises in previous years participate in Bible teaching on purity and attend the ceremony to support the first-timers.

In the coming year, thousands of churches will provide beautiful services built around promises of purity. Some churches won't. When churches go more than a year without inviting their students to settle this issue before God, they place those kids somewhat at risk. But parents and leaders can link arms to find God's timing for their students and families.

Does TLW Work Today?

All spiritual journeys are the exclusive work of God's Spirit. No teenager comes to Christ or makes a promise of purity unless God's Spirit empowers him. So the question is not, "Does True Love Waits work?" The proper question is, "Is True Love Waits consistent with what the Spirit is doing?"

Parents and leaders who don't understand the full message of True Love Waits might assume it's just kids signing cards and trying hard not to have sex until marriage. But True Love Waits is a process. While it includes the moment a promise is made, TLW also includes everything families and churches do to equip and encourage teens to live out that promise.

Sadly, True Love Waits sometimes means nothing more than a poorly-prepared lesson given during a single youth group meeting, followed by quick signatures on index cards that are left around the room. Few would expect that kind of commitment to lead to life changes. But when parents and church leaders, in the power of the Spirit, give their very best to offer preparation and support, the future often will be altered.

Criticism in the Media

Some parents and leaders have been confused by reports that indicate True Love Waits does not lead to lasting change. In recent days, some secular research has found a disappointing number of students who made some type of abstinence pledge, only to become sexually active later. But these studies lump together all students who have made any type of pledge or promise—including those who sign a pledge at school after only one or two health class presentations on disease and pregnancy.

If students make a quick pledge without the benefit of Scripture or the power of the Spirit, we shouldn't be surprised that they break these superficial "promises." Still, even though TLW commitments might make up only a small percentage of the total, those reporting these studies question the viability of True Love Waits. Further research focusing specifically on True Love Waits pledges needs to be done before any honest statements can be made about the movement's effectiveness.

Angry Opposition

It is interesting to note the vocal opposition to abstinence raised by many in government and academia. Some are expressing without reservation their belief that sex should be a joyful part of teenage living and that warning against early sex impinges on adolescent "rights."

A report in the *Journal of Adolescent Health* maintained that abstinence education is scientifically and ethically problematic. The authors claimed that teaching young people to postpone sex until marriage is "inconsistent with commonly accepted notions of human rights."[9]

Another story, published on LifeSiteNews.com, reported that one British health care expert "told media that as long as teens are fully informed about sex and are making their decisions freely as part of a 'caring relationship,' they have as much right as an adult to sex."[10]

Recently, government funding for abstinence education has faced dramatic cuts. In the public square, church leaders and parents have every right to weigh in on this issue since it never was the government's role to teach sexual values to children. Maybe an era of reduced focus on abstinence will challenge parents to step up to the plate. Maybe leaders now will again see a focus on purity from birth to marriage as central to achieving their mission.

The Big Picture

Sexual purity is a powerful way to acknowledge the supremacy of Christ. It lets students stand before God's throne and worship Him without guilt or shame. Purity is a clear response to Christ's majesty and His lordship.

Purity also allows students to accomplish kingdom work with passion and power. Avoiding diseases and not having babies as teenagers are good things, but they pale in comparison to a focus on bringing great glory to Christ as part of a generation that abides in Him in purity.

1. Elizabeth Landau, "Rise in teen birth rate may have been 'blip,'" CNN [online], 6 April 2010 [cited 20 May 2010]. Available from the Internet: *http://www.cnn.com/2010/HEALTH/04/06/teen.births.cdc/index.html*.
2. "True Love Waits in a Wedding Ceremony," True Love Waits [online], cited 21 May 2010. Available from the Internet: *http://www.lifeway.com/tlw/leaders/tools_wedding.asp*.
3. Bridget Maher, "Why Wait: The Benefits of Abstinence Until Marriage," Family Research Council [online], cited 21 May 2010. Available from the Internet: *http://www.frc.org/get.cfm?i=IS06B01*.
4. Christian Smith and Melinda Lundquist Denton, Soul Searching: The Religious and Spiritual Lives of American Teenagers (New York: Oxford University Press, 2005), 56.
5. Drucilla Dyess, "Pregnancies & Sexually Transmitted Diseases on the Rise Among Teens," HealthNews.com [online], 21 July 2009 [cited 21 May 2010]. Available from the Internet: *http://www.healthnews.com/family-health/sexual-health/pregnancies-sexually-transmitted-diseases-rise-among-teens-3478.html*.
6. Elizabeth Landau, "Rise in teen birth rate may have been 'blip,'" CNN [online], 6 April 2010 [cited 20 May 2010]. Available from the Internet: *http://www.cnn.com/2010/HEALTH/04/06/teen.births.cdc/index.html*.
7. Christine Kim and Robert Rector. "Executive Summary: Evidence on the Effectiveness of Abstinence Education: An Update," The Heritage Foundation [online], 19 February 2010 [cited 21 May 2010]. Available from the Internet: *http://www.heritage.org/Research/Reports/2012/02/Executive-Summary-Evidence-on-the-Effectiveness-of-Abstinence-Education-An-Update*.
8. Malcolm McDow and Alvin L. Reid, Firefall: How God Has Shaped History Through Revivals (Enumclaw, Washington: Pleasant Word, 2002), 334.
9. John Santelli, et. al, "Abstinence and abstinence-only education: A review of U.S. policies and programs," Journal of Adolescent Health, January 2006, Vol. 38. Issue 1, 72-81. Abstract available from the Internet: *http://www.jahonline.org/article/PIIS1054139X05004672/fulltext*.
10. Hillary White, "An Orgasm a Day Good for Health, National Health Service Tells U.K. Teens," LifeSiteNews.com [online], 15 July 2009 [cited 28 July 2009]. Available from the Internet: *http://www.lifesitenews.com/ldn/2009/jul/09071506.html*.

TLW 3.0:
PATH OF PURITY

BY JIMMY HESTER

The common way to identify a new edition of a computer program is through a numbering system (1.0, 2.0, and so forth). So, if we're introducing TLW 3.0, you might be wondering, *What was in 1.0 and 2.0 to build upon?* We're glad you asked.

TLW 1.0: Abstinence Until Marriage

When True Love Waits entered the picture in the early 1990s, society expected teenagers to be sexually active. The previously-held views of keeping sexual messages off television and the big screen and limiting them in advertising were challenged. The shift toward an open expression of sexuality led parents and their children to think that everyone was having sex. Meanwhile, abstinence was not presented as an option.

But not everyone condoned this shift toward a more sexually-explicit society. Christian parents and students expressed concern over teen sexual behavior and the stereotypes presented in the media. Their concerns were addressed through solutions centered around students, parents, and church leaders—and True Love Waits was launched. The initial True Love Waits commitment stated...

Believing that true love waits, I make a commitment to God, myself, my family, my friends, my future mate, and my future children to remain sexually abstinent from this day until the day I enter a covenant marriage relationship.

TLW 2.0: Holistic Purity

By the mid 2000s, the abstinence movement had gained momentum. Teens were becoming aware that abstinence was not only an option for their lives, but also the best way to avoid the consequences of bad sexual decisions.

But even as the emphasis took root, TLW began to recognize another shift in the abstinence discussion. "Purity" began making its way into the conversation, expanding the biblical understanding of abstinence. Many teenagers were publicly expressing a commitment toward purity in every area of their lives, not just their sexuality. In response, the wording of the True Love Waits commitment was adjusted to emphasize holistic purity:

Believing that true love waits, I make a commitment to God, myself, my family, my friends, my future mate, and my future children to a lifetime of purity including sexual abstinence from this day until the day I enter a biblical marriage relationship.

TLW 3.0: A Process Toward Lifelong Purity

In April 2009, student leaders in the sexual abstinence movement participated in a True Love Waits Summit in Nashville, Tennessee, to consider the future of TLW. Sessions focused on identifying specific challenges students faced, how parents and leaders could meet those challenges, and ways True Love Waits can remain effective for future generations.

The primary take-away from the Summit was the need for a greater emphasis on parental involvement, specifically finding ways church leaders can support parents in their role as the primary spiritual developers of their children. While society may encourage teen sexual behavior, the Summit participants noted that many parents live in a state of denial regarding the scope of the problem and the ways their children are affected. Issues identified by the participants included:

- ◆ dysfunction in families
- ◆ absence of parental supervision
- ◆ weak parental standards
- ◆ parents being reactive rather than taking preventive measures
- ◆ inconsistent lifestyle models at home

In response, the True Love Waits Team created *True Love Waits 3.0: Path of Purity*. This emphasis is a promise and a process toward a life of purity, including sexual abstinence until marriage. The path identifies a variety of life markers that one experiences from birth into young adulthood. Resources supporting TLW 3.0 guide parents and church leaders to take advantage of these markers and to treat them as teachable moments as they guide their children toward a lifelong commitment to purity.

Creating a Culture of Purity

Right or wrong, many people have viewed True Love Waits as an event—a one-time place where teenagers are challenged to sign commitment cards. It was never intended to be that simple and still be effective for the average student. Effective True Love Waits experiences include three steps: an educational element, a commitment element, and follow-up.

Students need to know why it is important to make a commitment to remain sexually abstinent until marriage (education). Armed with that biblical understanding, they can then make an informed decision about embracing purity and are more willing to do so (commitment). But it will not be easy to maintain the commitment without the ongoing support and encouragement of peers, parents, and other significant adults (follow-up).

If parents are going to create a culture of purity that will have a lasting impact on their children, certain puzzle pieces must come together, such as:

- Providing an environment for making a decision for Christ
- Celebrating markers during the developmental years of life
- Supporting and encouraging children in all aspects of development
- Providing an accurate, biblical education on sexual matters
- Promoting consistent church involvement
- Practicing parental supervision of their children
- Creating and engaging in intentional conversations
- Seizing teachable opportunities
- Practicing repentance and restoration when needed
- Providing accountability
- Partnering with church leaders for the good of the child

Path of Purity Markers

The foundation for creating a culture of purity is the child's decision to follow Christ as personal Lord and Savior. Beyond that, life markers represent building blocks for creating a culture of purity. We have identified 18 markers that provide parents (with the support and encouragement of church leaders) opportunities to lead their children toward a lifelong commitment to purity. These will be discussed in detail throughout this book, but a high-level view of each marker follows.

Childhood

1. **Birth and Infancy:** At birth children start gaining awareness of their personhood. A child's positive self identity is directly related to his ability to accept who he is. A young child builds trust with parents and caregivers.

2. **Physical Curiosity/Potty Training:** As children grow, they begin exploring their bodies and enjoy discovering new things. They constantly acquire information and actively listen to what they are being told about their bodies.

3. **Starting School:** In the early school years, children have an aversion to the opposite sex. School also begins their experience of gaining freedom to make choices—away from parents' constant care.

4. **Sexual/Social Development:** Older children begin to recognize physical changes in themselves and others. Interacting with the opposite sex becomes more common. They establish an awareness of body image. Initial sexual experimentation can begin to occur.

5. **"The Talk":** During the latter years of childhood, a child begins to question issues related to sexuality. Significant body changes, conversations with peers, and exposure to sexual material generate many questions.

Younger Youth

6. **Puberty:** Puberty is the point at which students are physically able to act upon sexual desire or temptation. Students begin to face pressure to be sexually active.

7. **13th birthday:** Around the 13th birthday, teens start seeing their peers and others act out sexually. They need to recognize the value of purity against the backdrop of an amoral culture.

8. **Entering the youth group:** Peer influence becomes a major factor in a teen's decision making and her search for acceptance. They could be exposed to pornography, "locker room talk," and impure relationships. This can happen both inside and outside the student ministry.

9. **True Love Waits ceremony:** This public commitment to purity helps students maintain strength and motivation to remain pure. Students need the accountability and encouragement that results

from the public support offered at this event. What happens before and after the ceremony should challenge both teens and parents to make a lifelong commitment to purity.

Older Youth

10. **Driver's License:** Getting a driver's license allows students to go places they never could have gone and do things they never could have done. Wise parents set boundaries, but they cannot be with their teenagers every moment of every day. Teens are left to make decisions, use proper discernment, and display trustworthiness.

11. **Dating:** When teens begin "going out," they also begin to face new temptations. What they've been seeing in the media and hearing from friends comes to life. They need to know how to have a relationship with a person of the opposite gender that doesn't compromise their commitment to purity.

12. **Exclusively Dating:** This is where teens begin to focus on dating only one person, but that level of commitment also increases the likelihood of sexual activity. The dynamics of the relationship, combined with normal physical development, increase the challenge to make wise, biblical decisions. Teens need to rely on a firm commitment to purity and accountability.

13. **Prom/Banquet/Formal:** This major social event leads many teens to make poor decisions—either deliberately or in the heat of the moment. Many teens see this as a "coming out" in which they dress and try to act more mature than they actually are.

14. **High School Graduation:** Children operate under the authority of their parents for nearly two decades. Graduation represents a shift to freedom for the student and "letting go" for the parents.

Young Adult

15. **College:** College students face situations that test their commitment to purity. They struggle with defining their core values and how those beliefs will be integrated into daily life.

16. **Singleness:** Singleness is not just an option for many young adults, it's their place in life. Maintaining purity in a society that expects everyone to be sexually active requires a deep commitment to God's plan.

17. **Engagement:** Many view engagement as "basically married," leading to a justification for premarital sex. A commitment to sexual purity provides accountability during this time.

18. **Marriage:** Marriage is a life-long covenant entered at the wedding ceremony. The husband and wife should be committed to one another and God to live purely in thought and action.

Path of Purity Detours

Along the path of purity, certain obstacles can sidetrack a successful journey. Some students will take these detours. Being aware of what lies ahead can help your child see warning signs and avoid danger.

◆ **Abuse:** Sexual and emotional abuse by a family member distorts God's intent for healthy family relationships. In many cases the abused becomes an abuser in adulthood. Sexual abuse by a peer through date rape or same-sex abuse creates deep emotional and social damage requiring professional counseling.

◆ **Sexual Activity:** Sex prior to marriage breaks God's laws and is a serious sin. It damages relationships between family and friends, erodes self-respect and respect of others, creates feelings of guilt and shame, and poses significant health risks (such as sexually transmitted diseases).

◆ **Pregnancy and Abortion:** Children deserve to enter the world under the best circumstances—free from disease, into a healthy family with married parents, and welcomed by everyone. Early sexual involvement can result in an unwanted pregnancy and its decisions and consequences.

◆ **Pornography:** Pornography can create a powerful addiction that attacks the mind and the body. It creates confusion about the true meaning of love and the rightful place of sex. It clouds issues of self-esteem and body image and devalues others for the sake of physical pleasure.

◆ **Homosexuality:** Homosexuality is often regarded as just an alternative lifestyle that has no impact on present or future relationships. Teens often explore same-gender sexual encounters without understanding the physical, emotional, social, and spiritual consequences.

◆ **Living Together:** Cohabitation is not God's plan for sexual expression. Couples who think they are finding intimacy without the commitment of marriage are really missing the true blessings of God's perfect design.

Parents, It's Up to You

TLW 3.0: Path of Purity can be a rewarding journey for parents and their children. But maintaining a healthy course relates directly to the commitment of parents to use every opportunity to guide their children.

PARENTS AND THE
PATH OF PURITY

BY BOB BUNN

The idea of a canal across Panama's isthmus wasn't new. Proposals and expeditions had been floating around for more than 300 years before a French company decided to take the plunge in 1880. But their planning was suspect, and their research was lacking. As a result, after 13 years and more than 20,000 deaths, France abandoned the project—unfinished.

A decade later, the United States picked up where the French left off, but the Americans learned from France's earlier experiences. Their planning and research were much stronger. They changed the canal plans from a sea level system to a lock system. They improved sanitation conditions to reduce the number of yellow fever and malaria cases. They provided newer technology and equipment.

And in August 1914, the first ship made its way through what one historian has called "The Path Between the Seas."[1]

Creating a path is never easy—whether it's a physical path that connects two oceans or a relational path that connects two hearts. It's hard work, but it's necessary work. And the results can be greater than anyone could imagine.

As a parent, your attempts to connect with the heart of your child may leave you feeling like the frustrated French in Panama. You're not sure where to turn. It's one step forward, two steps back. The emotional and spiritual wounds are deepening, and you're close to throwing in the towel.

First of all, remember that you're not alone. All parents—including the ones contributing to this book—struggle with the job God has given them. We've all felt lost, but the key is refusing to give up. The God who gave you this task will give you the strength and wisdom you need to complete it.

Whose Job Is It, Anyway?

A fair question to ask would be, "Is it really my job to be the primary spiritual developer of my kids?" It's fair because we don't see a lot of parents embracing that role these days. In some cases, well-meaning church leaders may even discourage parents from "dabbling" in the spiritual lives of their children.

But the Bible is clear that God expects parents to mentor their children in every aspect of life—including matters of faith. One primary passage where God reveals this truth is Deuteronomy 6.

The Book of Deuteronomy is really a series of speeches delivered by Moses on the brink of the promised land. In a sense, they are his "last words" to the children of Israel. They had been this close to Canaan before and missed the chance to enter because of disobedience (Num. 13–14). This time, Moses wanted to make sure the children of that stubborn generation avoided the mistakes of their elders. He wanted to remind them that God is faithful and would bless them if they would stay faithful to Him.

Moses' message in Deuteronomy 6 is really pretty simple. He called the Israelites to know God, own their faith, and make their faith known. In verses 4-6, he talked about confessing that there is only one God (knowing), putting God's words in their hearts (owning), and sharing these truths with future generations (making known).

And when he talked about making their faith known, he specifically talked about their role as parents. They were commanded to repeat God's message to their children and to communicate His truths in every possible setting (vv. 7-9).

Later in the chapter, he emphasized the role of parents again. When their children started asking spiritual questions, the parents needed to know the truth and be prepared to share it (vv. 20-25). Faith would survive as parents embraced their job as the primary spiritual developers of their children.

In contrast, the Book of Judges reveals what happens when that design falls apart. While "[t]he people worshiped the LORD throughout Joshua's lifetime and during the lifetimes of the elders who outlived

Joshua," a later generation arose that "did : works He had done for Israel. The Israelite LORD's sight" (Judg. 2:6-11a). Elsewhere, th "everyone did whatever he wanted" (Judg. God's plan, and chaos ensued.

So, God calls parents to focus on being ɛ children in every arena of life—including ɪ uncomfortable subject, it is a vital subject b Deanna Harrison point out in their book, F teaching your teenager about sex... So the q *to teach your teenager the truth about sex if you, ɪɪɪ̣ pɑ* ʋ*ɪ̇ɪɪ*, *ʷ* ʋ *ɪ̇* *ʋ*.

What Holds Us Back?

Admittedly, sexuality and purity are sometimes difficult to discuss. Even understanding that God created sex as a special gift to be shared inside a marriage relationship, it's tough to get that information out of our brains and past our lips. We think it's something "nice people" don't discuss.

While that might be true in a conversation with your Aunt Martha, purity is one topic you must discuss with your child—no matter how uncomfortable you feel. The first step toward talking with your child may be figuring out what's holding you back. Here are four common hang-ups parents struggle with related to purity and some truths to help you overcome those struggles.

1. **Fear.** You might simply be too embarrassed to talk about sex and purity, or you're afraid your child might be embarrassed if you bring it up. You also might be tempted to think that talking about sex will make your children more curious about it.

    Truth: The Bible says that God hasn't given us a spirit of fear (2 Tim. 1:7). That's not to say you'll be completely at ease talking about purity, but trust God to give you the strength to start the conversation. Refusing to talk about sex only limits your child's access to reliable information, forcing him to look elsewhere for the answers he needs.

2. **Confusion:** Perhaps your parents never talked to you about sex. If so, you really don't have a frame of reference for initiating a conversation with your own kids or explaining things in a way they will accept.

    Truth: The greatest fear many humans experience—even greater than a fear of death—is looking like a fool in front of others. That's why few people enjoy public speaking. But you don't have to look like a fool to your child. If you feel rusty on the basics of purity, find out what the Bible says about it. Read what reliable Christian writers

e research it takes to gain the knowledge you need. And
d hits you with a question you can't answer, admit it and
to find the answer. Your honesty will score points with her,
it leaves the door open for more conversations in the future.

pathy: Many parents tackle the question of sex by not tackling it all. They wonder why everyone makes such a fuss about purity because they don't see it as a problem. They live by the motto, "It'll never happen to my kid."

Truth: We've already touched on this principle, but it's worth repeating: *If you don't teach your teen about purity, someone else will.* If you don't do it, there's a good chance the information will come from someone who doesn't share the values you want your child to adopt.

4. **Guilt:** When it comes to sexual purity, a stroll down memory lane can turn into a nightmare on Elm Street for some parents. These parents weren't committed to purity when they were younger, so they can't imagine standing up for it in front of their children. They don't want to be hypocrites, so they remain silent as they wrestle with their own past.

Truth: If you struggle with sexual sins from your past (or present), let me share one word with you: *forgiveness.* God sent His Son to die so you could be forgiven. He promises to forgive anyone who genuinely confesses his sin (1 John 1:9). But you also need to know the word *repentance.* That means not only confessing your sin, but also turning away from it. You're only a hypocrite if you live like everything's fine while you refuse to stop doing what you know is wrong.

What Can We Do?

Even if you accept your role as the primary spiritual developer of your child and deal with fears that might hinder you, you still need a plan. Remember the difference between the French and the Americans in Panama? Creating a strategy for success and working at it is incredibly important. Here are some things you can do to begin your family's purity journey.

- **Begin as early as possible.** Even in infancy and childhood, you can teach purity and create a culture of communication by the way you deal with things such as bodily functions and potty training. As your child grows, you can build on that foundation with age-appropriate conversations about things like what they call certain parts of the body, how to protect themselves from predators, what to expect during puberty, and why sexual abstinence until marriage is so important.

- **Encourage communication.** If you wait until your child is a teen to sit down for a one-and-done talk about purity, the battle will be lost. You have to communicate across time with a series of conversations.

Again, age appropriateness is important, but start where you are right now. If you're behind, don't try to catch up in one sitting. Be sensitive to teachable moments and build credibility by listening more than speaking.

- **Make sure no question is off limits.** As a parent, you're the one to provide accurate information about purity. To be effective, you have to take *every* question as it comes.

  Most likely, your child is not trying to embarrass you or put you on the spot. He's simply looking for information. If you don't know the answer, admit it and promise to find out. But don't dismiss a question—and your child—because a touchy subject comes to the front.

- **Model purity in your own life.** Back in Deuteronomy 6, Moses told the Israelites to make sure God's words were in their own hearts first. Then, they could teach their children. The same is true on the path of purity. You can't lead anyone down a road you're not walking yourself.

  Your example is critical to your child's development, so be conscious about how you treat your spouse. Display love and appropriate affection. Teach your child through the way you interact with friends. Don't just talk about respecting others. Show your child how it's done.

- **Protect your relationship with your spouse.** God created us as relational creatures and to express intimacy within the confines of marriage. So, find time to nurture intimacy with your spouse—remembering that intimacy doesn't always mean "sex." Celebrate God's perspective on marriage and find quiet times to strengthen your relationship with each other.

- **Love your child even if true love doesn't wait.** If your child faces the consequences of sexual activity, stand at his or her side no matter what. Your hurt may be deep, but your child is hurting too. To lead her toward God's forgiveness and a second virginity, you have to model forgiveness yourself.

What If You're a Single Parent?

The marriage relationship provides an incredible sense of fulfillment and satisfaction. In many ways, it meets some of our most basic human needs. And when that relationship dissolves through divorce or the death of a spouse, that desire for personal affirmation and a sense of value doesn't just vanish. But trying to find fulfillment through sex outside of marriage is as much an illusion for you as it is for those who have never married.

As a single parent, you still have a responsibility to reflect God's design for purity in your life. You have to steer clear of detours like sexual activity and pornography so you can keep your family on the path of purity.

Single parenting is tough, but you can find support from God and His people. You also can find significant adults who can invest in the lives of your children. These individuals won't replace you or remove your obligation as a spiritual leader, but they can support the message of purity you are working to instill in your child's life.

Ready to Go?

You may agree that you need to be the one guiding your child on the path of purity. But you're thinking, "What do I do?" or "What do I say?" That's what the following chapters are all about.

Chapters 5-8 deal with different time periods in your child's life. Within each time period we've identified markers — significant events, experiences, or life stages that happen in the lives of most children. We see these markers as opportune moments to guide your child on the path of purity. With each marker we've given you the following information:

- **Marker descriptions** — a few statements to help you understand what is happening in the life of your child at this moment.
- **What your child needs to know** — things your child needs to be aware of that are taking place in or around him.
- **What you need to know** — information to help you understand what your child might be experiencing during this time.
- **Tips for what you need to do** — a few tips on how to help your child remain on the path of purity.

Not every child makes it down the path of purity unscathed. There are tragic experiences and bad decisions that could, and perhaps have, detoured your child. Chapter 9 will provide guidance for healing hearts, mending relationships, and steering your child back on the purity path.

The advice given here is not clinical instruction, but rather practical, conversational guidance from fellow travelers on the path of purity. Along the way you may feel overwhelmed and under-qualified. Trust me, you're not. No child has perfect parents, but God doesn't make mistakes — and He has chosen you as the parent of your children. In His scheme of things, you are the best person to lead your family on the path of purity. And He's promised to be with you every step of the way.

1. David McCullough, *The Path Between the Seas: The Creation of the Panama Canal, 1870-1914* (Riverside, N.J., Simon & Schuster, 1978), n.p.
2. Lynn Pryor and Deanna Harrison, *Pure Parenting* (Nashville, Tenn.: 2009), 9-10.

CHILDHOOD MARKERS

BY JEFF LAND

P salm 127:3 reminds us that children are a heritage from the Lord. In other words, your child is truly a gift, a precious trust. Jesus confirmed that in Mark 10:13-15, where He scolded the disciples for turning away children. Jesus welcomed children. He touched them, held them, and blessed them. They were a living illustration of the kind of trusting faith adults are supposed to have.

You probably already knew that. You understand the value of the child you held in your arms when she was born or have watched grow through the years. Of course, you also know the weight of responsibility that comes with the job of a parent. You are the primary spiritual developer of your child. Each day, you are making lasting impressions on her life. Your child is like wet, soft clay in your hands.

How will you shape her?

Purity Marker
BIRTH AND INFANCY

Emphasis: God's Design, Communication

1. Marker Description

You're probably wondering how birth and infancy have anything to do with leading your child on the path of purity, but this stage actually has a huge impact on your child's decision to choose to live a pure life. The sense of self-worth your child begins developing in infancy can teach him that he is a valuable part of God's creation. Your child also can learn early on that he is loved and can learn to respect himself.

As a parent, understand that at this time, your child...

- **Needs positive words and affirmation** (Gen. 1:27,31; Jer. 1:5). Think about how a new dad acts the first time he sees his little girl. He showers her with words about how beautiful and sweet she is. He tells her he loves her and that she's his pride and joy. Spoken in a sweet, soft tone, the baby recognizes that this is a voice she can trust. Helping your child feel special and loved should be a key goal for you during this stage of development. You can start instilling her value as a person created in God's image and with His plan.
- **Is becoming aware of his personhood** (Ps. 139:14). Watching a baby discover his hands for the first time can be entertaining. He may jerk his arms straight out and spread his fingers wide. He may practice making a fist or putting his hands in his mouth. He explores his body and discovers how to move his arms and legs. He starts holding his head up on his own and crawling—and will be walking before you know it! Helping your child discover that God made his body is an important part of leading him on the path of purity.
- **Establishes trust with parents and caregivers.** Child development experts say that establishing trust and attachment with your child is one of the most important things you can ever do for her. A child who

experiences healthy attachment will find life easier to navigate and will be more likely to develop as a secure, well-adjusted child. Children who are not attached are more likely to exhibit aggression, depression, developmental delays, and learning difficulties. Attachment is vital during your child's first three years of life.

- **Is learning how to feel comfortable with curiosity.** Her eyes are open wide, and she is bobbling her little head back and forth taking in everything and everyone she sees. Infancy is a time of constant learning. Every experience your child has increases her knowledge. She is learning about how to have relationships and how to interact with her environment. Your responses to her curiosity will teach her about when and how she can explore. Exposing your baby to colors, music, words, sounds, and tactile toys gives her an experience that affirms that it's OK to learn. Your child's learning styles and ability to process new information are being formed during this marker.

2. Your Child Needs to Know...

- **He is valued and wanted.** Humans are born with an innate need to be wanted. Babies need to feel cared for and loved. This is an important step in building attachment.
- **You will take care of all her needs.** Diaper changes, bottle feedings, sleeping, soothing, and playful banter — babies rely on others to take care of their every need. Whether it's as simple as walking your child around the room when she cries or changing her diaper when she is wet, she is totally dependent upon the care you provide her. This care and concern begins the process by which she learns to care for herself.
- **Consistent caregivers.** You are your child's primary caregiver at home, but what about while you are at work or church? Developing consistent relationships with people is an important part of your baby's attachment process. Work to ensure that you are providing your baby with as much consistency as possible.

3. What You Need to Do...

- **Talk to your baby.** The importance of providing positive affirmation cannot be emphasized enough. Especially in the beginning, you will not receive much confirmation that your baby is even listening. But you can be sure that he is beginning to connect your voice with your face. He is learning that he can trust you and depend on you. He is experiencing unconditional love, and this pattern will set into motion a relationship that fosters open and honest communication, dependence, and trust throughout his life.

- **Show affection.** Hold your baby. Hug your baby. Kiss her head, hands, and feet. Let her experience the warmth of your skin. Consider using a sling while you complete housework or go for a walk in your neighborhood. Physical touch and skin-to-skin contact are important factors in developing a strong bond. Your affection for your baby will begin to teach her that she is loved and valued. By touching her appropriately, she learns what feels good and how she should expect to be treated. While it may sound odd to teach your baby how her body should be treated at such a young age, each step you take today toward a positive environment sets the stage for future conversations.

- **Foster a healthy sense of trust.** It's important that your baby learns how to trust others. This is done by always providing a secure environment. Choose caregivers whom you fully trust. Always meet your child's physical, emotional, and spiritual needs. Provide consistency in scheduling, caregiving, and so forth.

- **Set appropriate boundaries.** The boundaries you set today correspond directly to your baby's ability to recognize boundaries later. These boundaries may range from how long you let him cry to who is allowed to change his diaper. Set a pattern of boundaries you can stick to so your baby can develop a healthy understanding of your authority. It can be quite annoying to hear a parent consistently say to a child, "If you do that one more time..." and then watch the child test the limits 10 more times. Start setting boundaries early. This will help him learn to set boundaries for himself as he grows into a child, a teenager, and even a young adult.

4. Tips for Fostering Attachment, Building Trust, and Setting Boundaries

- **Make time for physical connection.** Skin-to-skin contact is very soothing for your baby. Both mother and father should allow their baby to rest her head on their chests. The heartbeat rhythm can be soothing for the baby and provide a sense of calm and security.

- **Sing songs and tell stories.** It really doesn't matter how well you sing. It's the sound of your voice that comforts your baby and helps him to know you are there. He loves to hear you talking to him. He begins to recognize words like his name, *Mama*, *Daddy*, *love*, and *Jesus*. Repetition is key. While it may test parents' patience, repeating the same songs never gets old for babies. They know what to expect, and that knowledge provides security.

- **It's OK to cry.** Did you know that your baby's cries when you drop her off for Sunday School are a positive sign that she is securely attaching? It is important to choose caregivers who are consistent in your baby's life. Consistency is a necessary part of developing a secure attachment.

- **Don't let your baby cry it out.** You might have been advised to "just let her cry it out," but this method is not necessarily appropriate. Your baby cries as a way of communicating with you. Her cries are the only method she has for telling you she is hungry, needs a new diaper, or craves some attention. Your response to her helps build her trust in you. When you are quick to respond to your baby, you confirm that she can depend on you to care for her needs. This is effective in building trust with your baby.

- **Think security.** You would never do anything to hurt your baby, but not everyone is looking out for the best interests of your little one. Make sure that all caregivers—whether they are church members, day care providers, or babysitters—have been through a thorough background check. Ask questions and know that when you leave your child, he will be cared for in a safe environment.

- **Remember rules and regulations.** Boundaries are so important. From the very beginning of life, teach your child about following rules. Teach him about good touch, positive words, and security through your example. As he grows, he will begin to understand that rules are put into place for his safety. This will lay the groundwork for understanding how to set boundaries for his own body.

Purity Marker
PHYSICAL CURIOSITY/ POTTY TRAINING

Emphasis: *Open, Honest, and Simple Communication*

1. Marker Description
It's the time every parent dreams of. Gone will be those last-minute rushes to the store to buy diapers. You will be free! Or so you think. Potty training is a wonderful time marked by frequent trips to the bathroom, emergency exits from the highway for quick potty stops, and lots of accidents. But this is also a great time for you to continue your conversations about physical purity and for your child to begin identifying his or her special body parts.

As a parent, understand that at this time, your child...

- **Is a literal and curious thinker.** This fact carries many implications for parents that your own parents may not have recognized. Preschoolers do not think in abstract terms, so use correct names for everything you describe.
- **Has begun exploring his body** (Ps. 139:14). My son was obsessed with his belly button at this age. It is normal for your child to want to check and touch all parts of his or her body. He may touch his private parts frequently. He may also be curious about your body.
- **Enjoys discovering new things in her environment or her physical qualities** (Jer. 1:5). One day, my wife was driving with our son, whom we adopted from Taiwan, when he suddenly exclaimed, "Mama, my skin is brown!" Kids begin to notice similarities and differences between themselves and their peers during this stage of development.
- **Is constantly acquiring information.** Why? Why? Why? You'll hear questions all day long during this stage. Your child will ask how things work, or she will begin to gather the information herself. She'll take apart toys, investigate the environment, or look through books to find answers.

- **Actively listens to what he is told about his body** (1 Cor. 12:18). Because your child is a literal thinker, he absorbs everything you tell him about his body. If you tell him that his penis is a peanut, guess what he thinks it is!

2. Your Child Needs to Know...

- **Her body belongs to her.** Unfortunately, your child is growing up in a society where sexual predators do exist. It is very important to begin teaching your child about allowing people to touch her body. Teach her about good touches like hugs, high-fives, and pats on the back. Teach her that only certain people should touch her private parts and assure her that if anyone ever tries to touch a place that makes her uncomfortable, she should tell you.
- **Boys and girls are different.** Your daughter notices that there are certain things about her dad that are different. Tell her about the differences in boys and girls in very simple, clear terms. There's no need for great detail, but you should use anatomically correct terms.
- **How to care for his body and choose appropriate clothing.** You can teach your child to take care of his body by allowing him to assist in bathing himself and brushing his teeth. Help him make good decisions about what to eat. Teach him how to pick out his clothes. This age is a great time to begin teaching your son or daughter about appropriate modesty. If you allow your child to dress inappropriately at an early age, the situation may escalate to a point where you lose control by the time he reaches adolescence.
- **God made her the way she is on purpose.** God doesn't make mistakes. Your child might begin to notice that she doesn't color as well as her friend. You may have a child with special needs who starts to notice that he can't do things like the other kids can. It is important to teach her that she is fearfully and wonderfully made. God made her exactly the way she is for a purpose. Help her develop a good sense of her self-worth during this time period by frequently using words of affirmation and lots of positive touch.

3. You Need to Know...

- **Always use anatomically correct words.** It might make you uncomfortable to use words like *penis*, *vagina*, and *breast*, but using anatomically correct words will make your conversations with your literal-thinking preschooler easier. Using slang terms to talk about your preschooler's body parts will only confuse him.

- **Keep communication open and honest.** Answer your child's questions, but don't overload her with information. Many times she has a simple request for information, but in your fear of answering the question, you might give too much information. Never lie to her as a way to avoid the conversation, but don't answer more than was asked.
- **Allow kids to explore and discover gender roles.** It is natural for a child to want to explore and discover. Just because a boy tries on his mother's shoes does not mean that he has homosexual tendencies. This stage of development is marked by a lot of exploration and discovery. It is normal for boys and girls to want to attempt things that society sees as gender-specific. Never make a child feel she is bad or abnormal because she likes to play with balls more than dolls.
- **Teach your child about appropriate situations.** Talk about appropriate touch. It's not a fun topic to write about, and it is certainly not a fun topic to talk about with your child. But be willing to help your child avoid possible abuse by giving her the most information possible about how to avoid these situations. Help her know that there are certain places on her body that only a doctor, nurse, parent, or she can touch. Be careful not to scare your child, but stress the importance of appropriate touch. Also remind her that she should always tell you if someone touches her in an inappropriate way.
- **It's time to talk about differences between boys and girls.** Your child has begun to notice the differences between boys and girls, so it is important that you help him to begin understanding those differences. Again, this is not an in-depth conversation, but more of a general discussion using anatomically correct terms. The difficulty at this age is discerning how much information is too much. You should not burden your child with information he cannot adequately process. Therefore, it is important to give your child pieces of information that he can digest over a period of time.
- **Modesty can be learned by example.** Think about your own choices in bathing suits and other clothes as an example to your child. She will learn about appropriate dress through what you model.

4. Tips for Keeping Communication Open and Honest with Preschoolers
- **The bathroom is your friend.** Much of your conversation about body parts and the differences between boys and girls will occur in the bathroom. It is important to establish a safe and comfortable place for your child to talk about the questions he has about his body parts. Failure to do so could make for a really awkward outing to your favorite restaurant!

- **Use books and other resources.** There are many great children's resources that can help you have conversations with your child. You should feel confident in any resource that you share with your child. Since not all publishers will share your views on modesty and sexuality, always preview a book before you share it with your child. Also, contact your local department of children's services office, which offers a wealth of information on positive touch and inappropriate touch.

- **Play dress up.** Show your child by your example that it's OK to dress up and try different activities. Your child enjoys seeing you get in touch with your own inner child. Encourage her desire to explore and discover new things. This type of play can also be used to help her learn how to dress appropriately.

- **Don't panic.** Your child might actually ask you some questions to which you don't know the exact answer. It's OK to tell him that you need to think about it and that you will answer his question at a later time. Be sure to follow up with him about all questions to verify that you have answered things satisfactorily. Don't be angry with your child for asking a question or using terminology that may sound inappropriate. He probably heard the language at school, church, or even at home from a television show or commercial. Help him understand that the term is inappropriate and help him know another word to say in place of the inappropriate word.

Purity Marker
STARTING SCHOOL
Emphasis: *Boundaries*

1. Marker Description

Your child will spend a majority of his childhood in a classroom. School is where he will learn many things that you may or may not want him to know. Providing him with the tools to make the best decisions about processing and using this new information is key to maintaining your child's walk toward a lifestyle of purity. Helping him understand how to set appropriate boundaries will guide him as he begins to face more difficult situations in his life.

As a parent, understand that at this time, your child...

- **Begins to make decisions about his body.** Your child can determine what he will wear and how he will take care of his body. He is watching how his friends interact with their bodies. He also is paying attention to the way you take care of your body and will begin to emulate your personal hygiene habits.
- **Is learning about treating all people with respect** (Gen. 1:27-28). School might be the first time your child has a real opportunity to interact with people of a different race, culture, religion, or social class. She has mostly been exposed to differences through television shows, in the grocery store, or at church. But during this time in her life, she will begin to interact on a personal level with them. Any seeds of prejudice that have been sown into her will begin bubbling to the surface as these interactions occur.
- **Starts developing decision-making skills** (1 Cor. 6:12-13). Whether your child learns in a public school, a private school, or at home, she will have the opportunity to make decisions in which your input will not be involved. Helping her learn how to make good decisions will be an invaluable tool in her life. During this period she will decide which friends to play with, when to disobey, and how much she will tell you.

- **Has an aversion to the opposite sex.** It's always interesting to watch school-aged kids self-segregate — not on the basis of race or religion, but on the basis of gender. Boys will automatically be drawn to the boys' table and girls will move toward their own group. They have different maturity levels and really believe that their opposite-gender counterparts are infested with "cooties."

2. **Your Child Needs to Know...**
- **Proper techniques for caring for his or her body.** By this time, your child has most likely developed a sense of modesty, and he probably doesn't want you in the room while he is bathing. But he needs to know proper bathing techniques (even washing behind the ears!) and good teeth-brushing techniques. Because he will also begin spending time with friends and will not be in your constant care, it's important that he knows how to choose good food for his body. Teaching proper hygiene and supporting a healthy sense of self is key in helping your child avoid possible self-image disorders.
- **How to choose appropriate clothing.** It is important that your child feels good about the way she looks. The media and society will tell her that she must dress a certain way, so it is important that she feels confident in the way she dresses. Involve her in shopping for clothing. Your son will probably care less about what his clothes look like than your daughter; however, in recent years, boys have become more interested in looking stylish. Provide a good model by dressing modestly and letting your child talk to older kids and teenagers who also dress appropriately.
- **The difference between tattling and appropriate telling.** No one wants to be labeled a tattler, but some children are naturally more apt to tell you everything that anyone does. Sometimes being labeled a tattler will make your child more aware of his decisions and might discourage him from telling you important information. Sometimes tattling is just a cry for attention, but there are times when the information is of utmost importance. Help your child understand the difference by pointing out information he shares with you that is very important and other information that might be considered tattling.
- **The boundaries of trust.** Hopefully by now you have established an open, trusting relationship with your child. Your example has taught her what to look for in friends, teachers, and other adults who can be counted as trustworthy. She has learned that some people can be trusted more than others and that some people do not deserve her trust. It is important to remember that her trusting abilities are still being developed, so a

predator could still manipulate her. Therefore, you must maintain an active involvement in all of her relationships.

- **That disclosing uncomfortable situations and inappropriate conduct is important.** Unfortunately, kids tend to think that they will get into trouble if they share information about an abusive situation. Even though that sounds silly to mature adults, children fear they might lose your love if they disclose such a situation. It is important to talk to your child and make sure he understands that there is nothing he can tell you that will cause you to stop loving him.

3. You Need to...

- **Provide guidelines for modest dress.** From swimsuits to Sunday best, you need to be involved with helping your child look stylish, yet covered. Try walking through your local children's clothing store and discovering what's in style, then determine whether that clothing is appropriate for your child. Don't forget that your child is looking at the way you dress to determine how to dress. Your example means a lot to your child.

- **Teach your child about appropriate touch.** Because your child has reached a point where she is no longer constantly in your care or the care of a trusted caregiver, you must teach her about when touch is appropriate and when it is not. Help her to understand which parts of her body are private and should not be touched by someone other than herself, her parents, or her healthcare provider. Help her understand that if she is in a situation where she is being touched inappropriately, she should tell the person to stop and immediately tell a trusted adult.

- **Have a keen awareness of the child's environment.** Although your child will not be under your constant care and supervision, it is vital that you are always aware of where your child is and what he is doing. You should monitor your child's media intake and guard against inappropriate video games, television, clothing, music, and so forth. Maintaining an active awareness of where your child is and what he is doing will protect him from falling prey to purity stealers such as pornography and inappropriate conduct.

- **Listen carefully to what your child is telling you.** Your child may not have the correct words to describe an abusive situation, so listen very carefully to what she is telling you. She might speak in abstract terms about a situation with another person or she may transfer the situation that happened to her to another child as she tells you the story. Active and appropriate response to this information will show your child that you are listening to her and genuinely care about her best interests.

- **Know that example means everything.** Help your child discover how males and females interact. Show him what a godly marriage looks like through your example. If you are a single parent, teach him through hanging around friends with strong marriages and through your own dating habits. It's important that your child learns how men and women should act around each other, both inside and outside of a marriage relationship.

STARTING SCHOOL

4. Tips for Establishing Boundaries

- **Set consequences.** Your child must know that there will be consequences when she violates your rules. Whether it is using the Internet without permission, dressing inappropriately, or refusing to take a bath, your child must know that breaking the rules carries consequences. This will establish a healthy fear for your discipline.
- **Talk, talk, and talk some more.** Throughout the course of this book, you will read about the importance of open communication with your child. That's because this can't be stressed enough. Take the conversation deeper by providing situational talk and allowing him to describe how he would react to certain situations. This will provide a basis for open communication when it really matters.
- **Make a list.** Determine early what rules you will have for your child's interaction with peers. How will you react when she wants to go to a friend's home whose parents you have not met? It is important to explain those rules to her early so she knows the terms of her social interactions before she asks. This list of rules should also apply to whose car she may ride in, where she is allowed to go with friends, and what types of media she is allowed to watch and use. Clearly explaining your expectations ahead of time makes the conversation easier in the long run.
- **Establish a pattern of respect.** Your child learns his prejudices from both your words and reactions. Teach him that all people should be valued because they are created in God's image. Emphasize the importance of refraining from derogatory comments toward people of different races, faiths, and social classes. Help him know that he can (and should) love and value all people.

Purity Marker

SEXUAL/SOCIAL DEVELOPMENT

Emphasis: *Awareness of Physical Changes/Social Development*

1. Marker Description

Whoa! Where did that come from? You simply asked your son how his day was and he completely unloaded on you, ran to his room, and slammed his door. Or maybe your daughter is sobbing that her life is completely over because she can't find the right clothes to wear to a party. Don't worry, your sweet, lovable child will be back—eventually. Even before puberty kicks in completely, older children experience a time of rapid changes. Hormones cause physical and sexual changes that leave your child grasping for a sense of control. Peers and relationships begin to take center stage. These emotional changes can be hard to handle and could leave your child grumpy or sad one minute and happily bouncing off the walls the next.

As a parent, understand that at this time, your child...

- **Is recognizing some uncomfortable changes taking place.** Almost every pop culture television show has an episode in which one of the children experiences one of those physical changes. These episodes tend to be lighthearted, but the subject can be incredibly serious to tweens—those children moving out of childhood, but not quite into adolescence. Physical changes are very personal, as boys and girls measure themselves against their peers. Girls may begin to wonder if something is wrong because they haven't developed breasts. Boys who have started growing body hair won't take their shirts off around the pool. These early changes that serve as a lead-in for puberty can be very confusing and frustrating.
- **Begins to interact more with peers.** The same kids who teased each other for having cooties have now begun to notice each other. They no longer have the strong aversion to the opposite sex, and it might even be *en vogue* for them to "date" in a very casual manner. While

some preteens start experimenting sexually, this period is more about understanding that boys and girls can actually be friends.

* **Establishes an awareness of body image** (1 Thess. 4:3-8). Boys and girls are starting to worry about their physical looks during this stage. Shopping at the right stores and wearing clothes that make them look good are top priorities. There is an awareness of overeating, and many girls may start self-imposed diets to avoid being overweight.

* **Is bombarded by misinformation about sex** (Eph. 5:4, Ps. 101:3). If you haven't already started having age-appropriate conversations about sexuality, the time for the first "talk" is here. While that is covered more thoroughly in the next marker, it's important to note that locker room talk is already abounding for your tween. Cool guys are recounting their version of sex, while girls may be hearing that sex is a way to show her boyfriend real love and devotion. In recent years, this type of talk has focused on oral sex more than vaginal sex.

2. Your Child Needs to Know...

* **How to recognize unsafe/inappropriate situations** (1 Cor. 6:13,18-20). Your child needs to have a good plan for getting out of an unsafe situation. Start by helping her know what an inappropriate situation looks like. If she's at a friend's house and they begin drinking alcohol or playing a sexually-oriented game, she needs a way out without looking like a dork. Having a secret word or text phrase is an effective method. Establish boundaries for Internet use in your home. Help your tween know that pornography is dangerous and highly addictive. Educate her on the dangers of impurity and its effects on a person's physical, spiritual, and emotional life.

* **Techniques for avoiding temptations and diffusing peer pressure.** Internet pornography, as mentioned above, can devour your tween's purity. Place parental security measures on your home computer. Teach him specific rules for what he can and can't do while he is not under your direct supervision. These rules should include what video games he can play and what movies he can watch. The fear of looking like a nerd is a vicious problem on the path of purity at this age, so helping your preteen learn ways to handle peer pressure is invaluable.

* **How to make God-honoring choices about her body.** Don't just focus on sexual purity. Help her make good decisions in relation to her physical self. Think about other temptations she faces, such as drugs, alcohol, tobacco, television, and music. Some earlier points have encouraged you

to tell your child how to avoid these things, but you also should focus on developing your child's ability to make these choices on her own. If he is put into a situation where he is going to be offered a beer, does he know the consequences? Can she pick a God-honoring CD from the thousands of choices at the music store? This could be considered the "rubber meets the road" step, since it reveals if your child really "gets it."

3. You Need to Know...

- **The conversation is constant.** You are fully expected to be in constant communication with your child. The open and honest communication pattern that you establish with him will be invaluable as you navigate the path of purity over the next few years.
- **It's your job to explain what is happening to your child's body.** Don't rely on a health teacher to explain the early stages of puberty. Take responsibility for helping your child know that physical changes are perfectly normal. Help her to know that each person is an individual and may reach puberty at a different time. It's OK to be the first or the last. God made each person unique. Tell your child that it is OK to talk to you about questions he may have about his development. These conversations may be easier in a gender-specific setting (mom with daughter, dad with son). If you're a single parent with a child of the opposite gender, enlist a trusted relative or role model to help you with these conversations.
- **Address homosexuality and God's design for men and women.** The media has raised up homosexuality to the point where your child is exposed earlier to this lifestyle. Explain the biblical stance on male-female relationships and that homosexuality contradicts God's design.
- **Model appropriate male and female relationships.** The way you and your spouse interact with one another speaks volumes to your child as she begins developing friendships with the opposite sex. It is also important to note that she is watching how you interact with the opposite sex to learn what boundaries you believe are important.

4. Tips for the Sexual/Social Development Stage

- **Situational talk is your ally.** It might sound clichéd, but situational talk can ingrain proper responses to dangerous situations into your child's mind. Here are some sample "What if" questions:
  - ▶ What if you are at a party and someone offers you beer?
  - ▶ What if you are with a friend and he pulls a pornographic picture up on his cell phone?
  - ▶ What if you are teased in the locker room for being a virgin?

- ► What if you are offered a cigarette by a friend on the way home from school?
  - ► What if your friends tease you because you are wearing a one-piece bathing suit?
- ◆ **Think about some other "what ifs" that might threaten your child's purity.** Help her understand that a pure life is more than just a life free from sexual impurity. It is a lifestyle of physical, mental, emotional, and spiritual purity.

SEXUAL/ SOCIAL DEVELOPMENT

- ◆ **Get help if necessary.** If your child has expressed feelings that he may be homosexual, you probably need to get help from a trusted minister or Christian counselor. There are other times you will need help from professionals, such as if your child has been sexually abused, has become addicted to pornography or drugs, or has developed an eating disorder. Don't be afraid to reach out for help when it is in your child's best interest.
- ◆ **Use books and other trusted information sources.** It's difficult to explain the ins and outs of development, so don't try to go it alone. Find books and other information that will help your child gain a better understanding of what is going on in his body. It's also important that your child visit a doctor for regular check-ups to make sure his body is developing properly.
- ◆ **Be involved.** Always know where your child is and be as involved in her life as possible. Make every effort to attend ball games and practices. Know all of her friends and their parents. Develop a network of parents and agree that you all will always report any kind of inappropriate behavior to the parents of the children involved.

THE TALK

Emphasis: Open Communication

1. Marker Description

Admittedly, this is not a conversation that most parents relish. If we're honest, many of us have avoided it. At the very least we have tried to pawn it off on the other parent. However, this conversation is crucial to keeping your student on the path of purity.

As a parent, understand that at this time, your child...

- **Is recognizing differences between males and females.** It's becoming more and more apparent to your child that boys and girls are different.
- **Needs to understand that sexual attraction to the opposite gender is God-given** (Gen. 1:27-28; Song of Songs). Sometimes in our attempt to steer children/teens on the path of purity, we can make sex seem like a bad thing. We need to help our children know that sex is a gift from God, and it honors Him when it is expressed inside the context of marriage.
- **Needs to develop appropriate boundaries (emotional, physical, verbal) with the opposite gender** (Eph. 4:19; 1 Cor. 6:13). That time when girls think boys are yucky and boys are sure girls have cooties is probably over. Now is the time to talk about godly standards and appropriate boundaries for guy-girl relationships.
- **Needs to understand that the ongoing emotional and physical changes taking place are normal** (Luke 2:52). How scary it would be to notice your body changing and not understand what was happening. It's time for our children to understand the changes in their bodies and that they are not weird. They're just growing up.
- **Needs reassurance that he is uniquely designed by God** (Ps. 139). As your child moves from preteen into the younger teen years and notices the different stages of development in himself and friends, he needs to be grounded in the truth that he is a precious and unique creation of God.

2. Your Child Needs to Know...

◆ **His feelings and questions are normal.** Nothing about them may feel normal, but it is a natural part of development. He needs to know that every person who has ever lived has experienced similar feelings and questions. It is important to talk about them.

◆ **You are on her side.** Your child may feel that talking with you about sexual feelings and questions may be scary and uncomfortable, but she needs to know that you are a trusted place for information, guidance, and encouragement as she begins to navigate the purity waters. She needs to know that you are a safe place to bring all her thoughts and issues.

THE TALK

◆ **Who to listen to concerning sexuality and purity.** He can't rely on his peers or the media to be the source of accurate information about sexuality and purity. Your child will receive lots of messages about what is right and wrong from the world around him—including what is appropriate and inappropriate in the purity realm.

◆ **What you put in your mind stays there.** She needs to make good choices about what to watch, listen to, and read. You may be able to closely monitor her media intake at this point, but at some point, she will be on her own to choose. Equipping her to make wise choices is very critical.

◆ **Other trusted adults he can talk with about these issues.** You should do everything in your power to make sure you are the primary source of information for any question your child might have about purity. However, the reality is that at some point ahead you will probably become uncool, stupid, a control freak, old-fashioned, or any number of other things in your child's eyes. Any of those qualifications might make it difficult for him to talk with you. If that's the case, gently lead him toward people you trust and who will provide a voice of godly wisdom—someone he might be willing to talk to when he feels he can't talk to you. It's not too soon to lay the groundwork for those relationships.

3. You Need to Know...

◆ **Don't make light of your child for asking you sexually-related questions.** Sometimes our way of deflecting what's uncomfortable is to make light of it. If you do that with your child's questions, you risk shutting down communication in an area where he so desperately needs your godly guidance.

◆ **Be prepared for this conversation.** Make sure the information that you are providing is accurate and shared in an age-appropriate way. If a question surfaces that you can't answer, don't provide information you hope is correct. Put that topic on hold, research it, then provide the answer.

- **Create an atmosphere of trust where everything is open for conversation.** Help your child know he can ask you about anything and that nothing is taboo. Although some topics may be very uncomfortable, ignoring or stifling the conversation will only push him to find someone who is willing to talk about it. With that said, you can—and should— talk about all subjects within appropriate boundaries.
- **Recognize that "the talk" needs to be a series of conversations.** Hopefully, you have used several opportunities in earlier years to set the stage for this conversation. However, if you have not, don't let that keep you from beginning the conversation now... and continuing it in the future.
- **Carefully monitor the sexual messages your child is receiving.** At this point, you need to take a very active role in monitoring what your child is watching, listening to, and reading.
- **Always keep the door open for continued conversations.** Be available and willing to continue this conversation, whether it is a formal "let's sit down and talk" conversation or a teachable moment. Don't think that once you have "the talk" your work is finished.

4. Tips for "The Talk"

- **Set an intentional time and place for "the talk."** Most of the time, if it's not intentional, it doesn't get done. If your child is ready for this conversation, don't put it off. Set the time now and make it happen.
- **Choose a comfortable environment.** This may be a place at home, at the park, in the car, or so forth. One thing to keep in mind is that it needs to be a place that's private, where your conversation cannot be overheard. At a booth in your favorite fast food place may not be the best spot. You may want to think about where most of the best conversations with your child take place, as this may be the spot for your conversation.
- **Plan what you want to say, but be willing to deal with questions as they surface.** Some things to think about: *What topics do you want to make sure you cover? How are you going to start the conversation? What do you want to accomplish?* Have a plan, but don't be afraid to deviate from the agenda as the need surfaces. Don't just focus on the physical aspect of sexuality. A healthy conversation should also include the social, emotional, and spiritual aspects. Covering all these areas highlights the complexity of our sexuality.

- **See this as a conversation rather than a lecture.** Conversation says "Let's talk." Lectures say, "Shut up and listen." Which would you want it to be? A comfortable conversation sets the stage for more conversations to take place in the future.
- **Pray.** Ask God for wisdom and for an openness between you and your child. Ask God to prepare your heart and the heart of your child for this conversation. Ask Him to guide your words and thoughts.
- **Set the stage.** Remember, this is not a "be all, end all" talk. Set the tone for this to be a continuing conversation. Your goal is to extend the culture of conversation you have built over the years.

THE
TALK

Helpful Resources
FOR CHILDHOOD MARKERS

The childhood years open the door for the initial steps down the path of purity and set the tone for future walks together. For further help, here are some resources that might encourage you along the way.

- *Kids Ministry 101: Practical Answers to Questions About Kids Ministry*, (LifeWay Press, 2009): This is your one-stop book of answering questions like: How do I choose the right curriculum for my church?; How do I prepare a budget?; and How do I enlist volunteers? The book includes a CD-ROM for additional ideas, articles, and forms.
- *Super Duper Fun & Exciting Absolutely Thought-Igniting Bible Activities for Kids: Babies through Kindergarten Edition*, (LifeWay Press, 2010): It's packed with over 100 activities categorized by eight Levels of Biblical Learning™ concept areas for babies through kindergarten. You'll find an entire chapter filled with fun activities for Easter and Christmas holidays. Includes nine helpful articles along with leader training plans. Plus, a CD-ROM containing additional resources is tucked inside the back cover.
- *ParentLife* magazine: Every monthly issue gives parents practical ideas, devotions for children and preschoolers, and insights to help parents meet the responsibilities and celebrate the joys of parenting.
- *Raising a Modern Day Knight* by Robert Lewis (Tyndale House, 1999): A unique approach to helping a father shape his son into a man.

YOUNGER YOUTH MARKERS

BY MIKE WAKEFIELD & PAM GIBBS

Tweens and younger youth are caught between two developmental stages—childhood and adolescence. In some way, they might be feeling like they live in some sort of twilight zone. They are bombarded with mixed messages like, "Don't act like a little kid!" and "Stop trying to grow up so fast!" Other times they move quite freely between these distinct stages, and they are rarely bothered by the inconsistencies in their behavior or attitudes.

Often parents of younger youth feel trapped as well. To be honest, we're caught in *their* middle, too. We aren't sure how to respond to this new child who looks a lot like the girl we saw grow up but acts a lot like an older member of the youth group. Yes, raising tweens and younger youth can be a challenge. And keeping their steps true on the path of purity is no small part of that challenge.

PUBERTY

Purity Marker

Emphasis: *Celebrating Uniqueness*

1. Marker Description

Coming of age is an interesting, wild ride that your younger teen doesn't need to take alone. The physical changes that began as a preteen will accelerate as he moves into adolescence, and these changes can be disturbing if experienced without proper preparation and support. He needs someone to walk with him through this crazy time and help him understand what is taking place. And you're the best person to help him.

As a parent, understand that at this time, your child...

- **Will be experiencing several body changes related to physical maturity.**
  For guys, changes include:
    - Maturation of sexual organs
    - Body, facial, and pubic hair
    - Deepening of the voice
    - Body odor and acne
    - Physical growth
  For girls, changes include:
    - Breast development
    - Maturation of sexual organs
    - Start of menstruation
    - Physical growth
    - Body and pubic hair
    - Body odor and acne
  In general, girls start the puberty stage earlier than guys — girls around 10, guys around 12.
- **Is reaching a point where he is physically able to act upon sexual desire or temptation.** This may be difficult to hear, but your child is leaving childhood behind and is now physically able to reproduce.

- **Facing pressure to be involved in sexual activity.** Perhaps for the first time, students will begin to hear about and be exposed to the pressure to be sexually active.
- **Is getting attention from the opposite gender.** This is especially true for girls who mature early, who might be noticed by older guys.

2. Your Child Needs to Know...

- **It is normal for his body to be changing at its own pace.** Your child will begin to notice that he is different than the other young teens. And whether he is maturing faster or slower than his peers, he will inevitably make comparisons and feel odd or weird. If he develops slowly, he may feel inferior. If he is an early developer, he may feel like a freak who is bigger and taller than his friends. In some cases, early development may lead to feelings of superiority, which can lead to bullying.

PUBERTY

- **God has made her unique.** The truth of God as Creator needs to be stressed amid the changes and comparisons. Your child needs to understand that she was not an accident or mistake. God designed her beautifully with a purpose in mind. *Odd* and *weird* are not in God's vocabulary when it comes to His creation.
- **Your child shouldn't be embarrassed by developmental differences.** Your daughter will have friends whose breasts are developing while hers are not. Your son's voice remains squeaky while his friends' sound mature. Whatever the difference, it can be cause for embarrassment.
- **He can talk to you about what is happening.** Continue to provide an atmosphere of trust and security so that your younger teen feels safe talking with you about what he is experiencing. And if the truth be known, he really does want to talk with you.
- **Why she shouldn't act on newly developing sexual desires.** It's OK to have the feelings because God put them there. But it's not OK to act on them. As she is learning about the physical changes that are producing the desires, she also needs to know about the biblical standards God has given us for holy living, especially in the area of sexual purity.

3. You Need to Know...

- **Puberty is happening at younger ages now.** In 1900, the average age for the starting of menstruation was 15. By 2002, it was 12.34. The onset of puberty is creeping younger, so don't wait until your child is 14 or 15 to have this conversation.
- **At this point, many teens begin dealing with body image issues.** Your self-confident child may suddenly become a self-conscious teen. Be

aware that body image can become a big deal as she begins to compare herself with peers. Your consistent encouragement and affirmation will offer a much-needed boost.

- **Students may be physically, socially, or emotionally awkward.** You may want to put bubble wrap around anything that is breakable because there is a good chance your growing son's big feet are going to trip over it and break it. You may also cringe as your child says or does annoying things just trying to fit in. Be patient. Puberty can be a very awkward time. Just keep that in mind and help pick your child up when they stumble.
- **Be aware that guys who develop later often become the targets of bullying and harassment.** Studies show that bullying is more likely to take place in younger teens than older teens. Here are some signs that your child may be the victim of bullying:
  - Comes home with torn, damaged, or missing pieces of clothing, books, or other belongings
  - Has unexplained cuts, bruises, and scratches
  - Has few, if any, friends with whom he spends time
  - Seems afraid of going to school, walking to and from school, riding the school bus, or taking part in organized activities with peers (such as clubs)
  - Takes a long, "illogical" route to or from school
  - Has lost interest in school work or suddenly begins to do poorly in school
  - Appears sad, moody, teary, or depressed when she comes home
  - Complains frequently of headaches, stomachaches, or other physical ailments
  - Has trouble sleeping or has frequent bad dreams
  - Experiences a loss of appetite
  - Appears anxious and suffers from low self-esteem
- **Students begin to sexualize their behavior because of what they see in culture.** Through media, peers, and other sources, your child is receiving plenty of sexual messages. Many of the messages will conflict with the godly standards you're trying to instill. You can't completely shield your child from wrong messages, but you can continue to monitor the sexual messages your teen is receiving and discuss them.
- **If little conversation has taken place about sexuality, it needs to happen now.** If discussions with your child about sexuality have been basically non-existent, don't wait any longer. Find time now to talk with him or her. Review information from "The Talk" marker to help with this needed conversation.

- **Talk to your child about a trusted adult she can talk to if she doesn't feel comfortable speaking with you.** During this time your child needs to be talking to a trusted godly adult. Hopefully that is you. But there may be times when your child will need someone else. Help her know who those kinds of people are: her pastor, student minister, Sunday School teacher, trusted friend, or another godly adult.

4. Tips for Handling Puberty

PUBERTY

- **Be informed about puberty.** Research the changes that take place in puberty so you have a better understanding of what is taking place in your child.
- **Discuss the changes that are happening — or will be happening — with your child.** Lead a frank discussion about what is/will be happening in his or her body. Things to cover:
  - ▸ The specific changes that will take place
  - ▸ Menstruation (with your daughter)
  - ▸ Timing of these events
  - ▸ How peers will react — both positively and negatively
  - ▸ Uniqueness and value as God's creation
- **Constantly affirm.** There will be plenty of people, situations, and conversations that will chip away at your child's self-esteem. Constantly encourage and affirm who your child is as God's creation. Tell him that you love him and are proud of him just because of who he is.
- **Move through this time in celebration mode.** Help your child understand that puberty is a good thing, a part of the passage from childhood into adulthood. Going through puberty is probably not something you want to announce to the world, so this should be a private celebration. Here are some ideas...
  - ▸ A mother-daughter outing. Think shopping, spa, hiking, horseback riding, tea party, or other things that interest your daughter.
  - ▸ A father-son outing. Think fishing, ball game, camping trip, hiking, or other things that interest your son.
  - ▸ This outing can still take place if you are a single parent. Even if your child is of the opposite gender, you can still find an activity both of you can enjoy. Use that as a basis for your celebration.

13ᵀᴴ BIRTHDAY

Emphasis: *Becoming an Adult*

1. Marker Description

In some cultures, this particular birthday represents a significant marker, a true rite of passage. This is especially true for young men. That's one of the reasons we focused the emphasis on becoming an adult. Perhaps it is at this point that you can intentionally begin to turn your child's focus from childhood toward adulthood. It is certainly appropriate for you to begin using terms and phrases such as "becoming an adult" and "young man" or "young woman."

As a parent, understand that at this time, your child...

- **Can understand the idea of leaving childhood and entering a stage where more is expected, more responsibility is given, and certain rights are bestowed** (1 Cor. 13:11). As you talk about this turn toward adulthood, be sure to talk about new privileges, but don't leave out the added responsibilities that come with the privileges.
- **Faces new challenges and problems.** Your student will not only experience peer pressure on issues such as sex, drinking, school work, success, and skills, but he or she also will feel pressure to fit in and be accepted. Things that might make your teen stand out as different have a tendency to be highlighted by peers.
- **Begins seeing peers and others act out sexually.** Sometimes this happens even earlier, but teens generally are starting to hear about, and perhaps even see, their peers begin to experiment with sex.
- **Might observe—and perhaps experiment with—same-sex attraction.** You probably don't want to read or think about this, but it is happening. There are even students who are "coming out" at this age. This possibility should prompt you to discuss the issue of homosexuality at this time. Your teen is aware of it, so talk about it in a biblical context.

2. Your Teen Needs to Know...

- **How to evaluate the status of his relationship with God.** This is a good time to nail down where your teen is on his spiritual journey. If he committed his life to Christ at a young age, discuss the reality of that decision. Is he certain of his salvation? If not, discuss why not and help him nail down this decision. If salvation is secure, then what is your teen doing to grow as a Christian? If he has not yet accepted Christ, make sure he understands the gospel and the need to make this most important decision. Don't push or force, but provide the opportunity for him to commit his life to Christ.

- **She is leaving childhood and entering a new phase of life, the teen years.** Intentionally talk about turning the corner from childhood to adulthood.

13TH BIRTHDAY

- **He is responsible for his actions and should recognize that the decisions he makes carry consequences.** Most teens want to focus on the added privileges that come with being a teen. However, you need to help balance that with reminders of the added responsibilities that come with this age. Plus, your teen needs to understand he will now be faced with decisions that carry greater consequences.

- **Feelings toward the opposite gender are beginning to change.** The icky boys are becoming cute, and the yucky girls are turning heads. This is normal, but it needs to be kept in perspective.

- **Just because her peers act out sexually, it does not mean it is healthy for her to do so.** Our society portrays sexual activity among teenagers as the norm. Even worse, your teen will become aware of friends who are sexually active. If so, she needs to know that what she sees and hears about sexual activity is not the standard unless it lines up with the biblical design for sexuality.

- **You are on his team to help establish personal sexual boundaries based on biblical principles.** Remind him often that he is not going to be left alone to navigate the sexual waters. You will be there to help identify, set, and enforce godly standards.

- **Recognize the value of purity and take practical steps to guard your teen's walk on the path of purity.** You can do this by teaching your teen to develop accountability relationships, avoid pornography, and guard what she brings into her mind. She needs to take control of the sexual messages that she is receiving. She certainly can lean on you and learn from you, but the responsibility to live according to godly standards needs to rest on her.

3. You Need to Know...

+ **That the physical changes of puberty will mirror relational changes you will experience as your child moves from childhood to adulthood.** You may have many moments when you wonder, "Where did my sweet little child go?" That is not unusual. Cherish the past, but open yourself to the joys of parenting a teen.

+ **While it may become more difficult, keeping an open channel of communication is essential during this stage.** Just know that you may have to work harder at communicating with your teen. But don't give up because it's hard. She needs (and wants) your voice of support and direction in her life. Watch for teachable moments.

+ **Understand that despite your best efforts to monitor sexual messages, your teen has received them.** You cannot completely insulate your child. Just keep the lines of communication open so you can discuss what he is hearing and the truth of those messages. Remember that you remain the most important voice in his life.

+ **The issue of masturbation often begins to surface at this age.** This may be a very uncomfortable subject, but you need to discuss it with your teen. While this is a common issue for boys, it is an issue that is becoming more common among girls.

+ **Teaching your teen to make wise choices is your responsibility.** Most times it's easier and less harrowing to make all the decisions for your teen. But if you do that, you have failed at one of your top priorities — equipping your child to be an independent adult who makes godly, wise choices. If you haven't already started that equipping process, now is the time.

4. Tips for This Marker

+ **Celebrate this time in your teen's life.** You may want to host a party with his friends and some family members. Or you might choose to mark this occasion with a celebration that intentionally focuses on his passage from childhood into young adulthood. Some parents choose to conduct a special celebration with just family members and a few adults who are significant to their teen. Often, they ask those significant adults to provide letters of encouragement to the younger teen that talk about what it means to be a godly man or woman. You can expand this idea for other significant birthdays, such as when your child turns 16 or 18.

+ **Discussions on these topics need to take place:**
  ▸ **Spiritual condition:** Talk about your teen's personal salvation. If your teen has already accepted Christ, revisit when he made

that decision. Make sure your teen has a good understanding of his commitment. Deal with any doubts that surface. Also discuss what your teen is doing to grow in his or her faith (quiet time, prayer, Bible reading, etc.). Encourage your teen to continue to grow in Christ.

▸ **Masturbation:** The Bible does not speak directly to this issue, so you may need to sort through your own feelings and beliefs first. Some parents feel it is inappropriate in all situations. Others think it might be acceptable as a normal part of growing up and as a way to release sexual tension. You will need to determine what is best and right according to your biblical values and principles. It definitely becomes wrong when it becomes an obsession and dominates your life. It is also wrong when it involves pornography and lustful thoughts.

13TH BIRTHDAY

▸ **Homosexuality:** Take time to explain homosexuality. Discuss what the Bible says about it in contrast to what the world says about it. Provide an atmosphere where your teen feels safe to discuss this and other potentially difficult topics. Be careful not to preach, but to share truth in love. Try to leave the conversation open for more discussion when needed.

◆ **Use your child's 13ᵗʰ birthday to mark new privileges and responsibilities.**

▸ **Possible new privileges:** later bedtime, more computer time, bedroom of his own, cell phone, pet, and so forth.

▸ **Possible new responsibilities:** baby-sit younger siblings or complete household chores (increasing number and/or difficulty). Some privileges add responsibilities of their own—such as getting a phone or a pet.

◆ **Set the example for healthy sexuality by demonstrating appropriate affection in front of your child.** You are setting the example of how to treat the opposite gender and appropriate ways to show affection.

Purity Marker
ENTERING THE YOUTH GROUP

Emphasis: Peer Influence

1. Marker Description

Probably up to this point in your teen's life, you have been the most dominant influence. Your voice has rarely been challenged. That is quickly changing as your teen begins listening to the voices (and actions) of her peers. As your teen enters the youth group at church, her world expands to include many more opportunities to interact with peers. This is not necessarily a bad thing, just a potential challenge as you navigate the waters of peer influence.

As a parent, understand that at this time, your child...

- **Is learning to discern what is true** (Phil. 1:9-10, Heb. 4:12). As the big, wide world begins opening to your teen, he is having to determine more on his own what is right and wrong.
- **Is looking to peers for affirmation** (Gal. 1:10). As much as you affirm your teen and encourage her to find her worth in who God made her to be, she is going to look for acceptance and affirmation from peers.
- **Faces increased temptation and pressure from peers** (1 Cor. 15:33-34). Along with the search for acceptance comes the dreaded pressure exerted by peers to conform.
- **Thinks peer relationships need to be more influential than parental relationships.** Sorry. I know you were probably hoping this wouldn't happen, but it usually does. And because it does, it's very important that you provide opportunities for your teen to be around students who are going to be a good influence.
- **May be exposed to pornography, obscene language, locker room talk, and impure relationships.** Your teen's exposure to impure things is probably increasing. You are able to control some of the exposure by monitoring some of the media messages, but not all of it.

2. Your Teen Needs to Know...

- **No one is above impurity, regardless of the environment.** Keep your teen from thinking, "That won't happen to me." If sexual sin can happen to a man after God's own heart (2 Sam. 11), it can happen to any of us. That's why we make commitments to sexual purity and then do everything we can to guard that commitment.
- **His relationship with you will probably change during this time.** This is not always a negative thing. In fact, the relationship needs to change as your teen moves from childhood to adulthood. Despite the change, he still needs to listen to your wisdom. Pray he would not value his peers' advice and influence over your counsel.
- **Resisting temptation is a lifelong discipline** (1 Cor. 10:13; Jas. 4:7). Your teen needs to know that choosing now to be pure will reap benefits later (Gal. 6:9). But the opposite is also true—choosing to be sexually active can lead to tragic consequences (Hos. 8:7).
- **She can trust you and other spiritual leaders that God has placed in her life.** Your teen will be looking for people she can trust. Do all you can to maintain your position as the person she can trust the most.
- **He should do what he knows is right, not what his peers expect of him.** Help your teen make decisions based on biblical standards and then be confident in them.
- **Set godly standards for the types of friends she has.** Encourage and guide your teen to choose her friends wisely.
- **Spiritual disciplines such as Bible study, prayer, Scripture memorization, and church involvement are important for spiritual growth and solid footing on the path of purity.** Maintaining a pure life is hard enough, but it's next to impossible without maintaining a growing relationship with Christ.

ENTERING
THE YOUTH
GROUP

3. You Need to Know...

- **Students at this age are becoming heavily influenced by their peers both inside and outside the church.** They look to their peers for what is the accepted and correct thing to do.
- **It is important for you to maintain communication with your teen about his choice of friends.** You want to give guided freedom. You don't want to pick your teen's friends for him, but you do want to influence his understanding of how to choose friends wisely.
- **Don't be surprised if your teen becomes less communicative.** Your child is becoming the one-word, one-phrase wonder. The extent of her responses to you may be "Fine," "OK," "I don't know," and

so forth. She may even respond with some abbreviations usually reserved for instant messaging, like "IDK" for "I Don't Know" or "BRB" for "Be Right Back." You also may notice her eyes glazing over when you're trying to talk to her. Even if it seems she isn't listening, continue to lovingly speak truth to her.

- **Formal conversations may decrease, making teachable moments more important.** The times when you can sit down to talk may become less frequent. However, you still will have many opportunities to teach and influence through teachable moments.

- **Though your influence may lessen, you are still the most important influencer in your teen's life.** Granted, your No. 1 ranking may seem a bit shaky, but you can and should remain the biggest influencer of your teen. She may indicate that she doesn't really care what you say, but that's not the case. Teen polls continue to show that a parent remains the biggest influence in a teen's life.

- **At times your frustration will threaten to overrule your judgment.** No doubt you will face some frustrating and trying times as a parent of a teenager. Don't throw in the towel! At times you will need to step back, take a deep breath, and ask, "What is the wise thing to do in this situation?" You will have to pick your battles and realize that not everything is a hill to die on.

- **Remember, you're the parent, not the pal.** Many parents derail the power of their influence because they try too hard to be their teen's friend, rather than his parent. It's not that you can't be friends with your teen, but be his parent first.

4. Tips for This Marker

- **Discuss the differences between what your teen hears from many worldly voices, including friends, and biblical truth.** Don't leave it to your teen to figure this out by himself. Talk about what he is hearing. Choose some of the current media, like the radio Top 10 or the hottest movies, and evaluate the message of each one. You can ask, "What do your friends think about this movie (song, book, etc.)?" Don't dominate the conversation. Focus on listening.

- **Take advantage of teachable moments to communicate truth.** Teachable moments happen in different places for different teens. When I was a teen, it happened when my dad and I were fishing or working in the garden. For you it might be in the car, at the dinner table, or during the last moments before bedtime. Whenever they are, take advantage of them to impart wisdom.

- **Do your best to eat at least one meal a day as a family.** Teens need order and routine. This simple step can help your teen feel more safe and secure. This will also provide a great time for conversation.
- **Resist the temptation to be your teen's friend rather than her parent.** Sometimes it's not fun being the bad guy. But you are the God-given authority in your teen's life. She is looking to you to set the boundaries for what is safe and right. Don't abdicate this role!
- **Remind your teen that every battle he wins over temptation is a big step toward a rewarding life of purity for himself and a future mate.** Help your teen keep the goal in mind. Continue to remind him that there is much more life out there than the teenage years.
- **Make your house a safe place for teens.** Make sure your teen knows her friends are welcome at your house. Getting to know your teen's friends and providing them a safe place to hang out is probably worth some crumbs and cola on the carpet. This doesn't mean you hover over them and try to be a part of every conversation. Let your presence be known occasionally, but give them some space as well.

ENTERING THE YOUTH GROUP

Purity Marker
TRUE LOVE WAITS CEREMONY

Emphasis: *Accountability*

1. Marker Description

The True Love Waits ceremony is a special event on the path of purity. While it can happen at any age, it's been placed in the younger youth section in the hopes that making an early commitment to purity will set a solid boundary for the rest of the teen years. Please understand that this ceremony is not the be-all, end-all moment for assuring your child remains pure. It is a significant moment, but it needs to be preceded by a commitment to follow Christ and purity marker moments before and after the ceremony. The emphasis and activities surrounding this event provide you with great opportunities to discuss purity with your child.

As a parent, understand that at this time, your child...

* **Needs to make a public and informed commitment to a lifelong pursuit of purity, including sexual abstinence prior to marriage** (1 Thess. 4:3-8; Heb. 13:4). You may be thinking, "My baby's too young to make this commitment. He doesn't even know about such things." Perhaps that's true for some students, but for the majority, sex is something with which they are all too familiar. Our society bombards us with sexual images and messages, plus what your teen is hearing among his peers. It's not too early.
* **Needs the support of both parents and church leaders to make and keep this commitment** (Deut. 6:4-9). The TLW commitment is not made in a vacuum. Your teen will need you to help hold her accountable. Hopefully your church will also support her commitment, by having a church-sponsored ceremony. If not, plan one within your own family or enlist other parents of teens to be involved in conducting a ceremony.

2. Your Teen Needs to Know...

- **The pressure to become sexually active demonstrates the need for him to make a public and reverent commitment to sexual purity.** This decision is not based on peer influence or public opinion.

- **Committing to sexual purity is an act of worship as she offers her life to God for His use.** The ceremony is not just an event where your child signs a card, gets a ring, and goes about life. It is a sacred moment where she devotes herself to walk in holiness in the area of her sexuality.

- **The pledge to sexual purity is an ongoing commitment, not a one-time event.** Help foster this truth with your child. The pledge will not shield her from the pressure to be sexually active that she will continue to face. The pledge will provide a commitment to stand on when pressures present themselves.

- **A True Love Waits pledge is a promise to remain pure in every area of life (body, mind, emotions, and speech).** Some want to limit the pledge to sexual intercourse. The commitment is much deeper than that. Your child needs to understand that he is committing to a life of purity in all areas: thoughts, emotions, body, and speech.

TLW CEREMONY

- **As a part of the commitment to sexual purity, your child agrees to keep the True Love Waits pledge and to be held accountable by parents and fellow believers.** If the commitment to purity is not followed up with encouragement and accountability, keeping it becomes much more difficult.

3. You Need to Know...

- **This commitment should be made within the context of an ongoing discussion about sexual purity.** Discussing your teen's participation in a TLW ceremony should not be the first discussion you have with him about sex. The ceremony has the potential to be a little overwhelming, especially if the service is a church-wide event.

- **Encourage your student to be involved in a True Love Waits ceremony.** Just because this marker is in the younger youth section does not mean you should push your younger youth to make this commitment. Discuss it with her. Make sure she understands the meaning and depth of the commitment. Do your best to answer all her questions about the commitment and ceremony. Gathering information on what will take place in the ceremony may help put her at ease about participating.

- **Some of your student's peers may not have parental support in the home.** Offer to be a "stand in" support and role model for them during the ceremony and after it.
- **Develop accountability for both you and your spouse to help ensure sexual purity.** Use this time to renew your own commitment to sexual purity and set up accountability for yourself. Remember, you are the most influential example to your teen.

4. Tips for the True Love Waits Ceremony
- **Support your student by being an active participant in the ceremony and by providing a significant token (such as a purity ring) for her (and possibly for yourselves) to commemorate this event.** This is a significant event you need to mark in a tangible way. There are rings and other jewelry available at *www.truelovewaits.com*. The significant token doesn't have to be jewelry. It can be another kind of token to commemorate your teen's decision and to use as a reminder of the commitment she has made.
- **Evaluate your commitment to purity in all areas of your life (mind, body, speech) and commit to setting the example for your student from this point forward.** The best encouragement for your child to live a life of purity is to see you living one. The True Love Waits ceremony is a great time for you to make a recommitment to live a pure life. If you've slipped along the way, it's also a good time to seek God's forgiveness. The Bible reminds us that God is faithful to forgive those who confess their sin (1 John 1:9). This would be a great time for you to find forgiveness and to renew your commitment to the path of purity.
- **Create a plan of support and accountability that will focus on the home.** Every family is different, and that's OK. This plan should be unique and tailored to fit what's going on in your home. Remember that the True Love Waits ceremony is not an end in itself. It really is the beginning of something very cool for you and your teen. For the commitment to stick, your child will need a great deal of encouragement and accountability from you.
- **If your church or student ministry doesn't have a ceremony planned, talk with your church leaders about planning one.** In chapter 10, you'll read more about creating a special partnership with the leadership of your church, but this ceremony represents some great common ground for initiating that partnership. Speak with your student minister or pastor about conducting a True

Love Waits ceremony. This could be a public commitment and celebration service for students and parents who are making the True Love Waits commitment. The ceremony could be an entire service or a significant portion of a service — with time allowed for testimonies, commitment, and commissioning. If the church is unable or unwilling to do so, perhaps you could lead a group of parents to conduct one.

TLW
CEREMONY

Helpful Resources
FOR YOUNGER YOUTH MARKERS

The transition from childhood to adolescence represents a period of incredible joy, marvelous memories, and more than a hint of confusion and fear. Some of that confusion rests in the hearts and minds of younger youth who aren't sure which step to take next. Some of it rests inside parents who see their "children" slipping away and aren't sure how to respond. Here are some resources that will help you understand some of the issues you will be facing as your child moves through the younger youth markers on the path of purity.

- *Living with Teenagers* magazine: This monthly magazine equips parents to raise teens who know God, own their faith, and make their faith known.
- Heart Connex, *www.heartconnex.com:* Designed for the busy family, these free, 20-minute Bible study devotions come via e-mail and are designed to involve both students and parents.
- *Designed by God* by Pam Gibbs (LifeWay Press, 2004): This study helps students understand homosexuality from a biblical perspective.
- *Complete: A Life of Purity* by Mike Wakefield and Pam Gibbs (LifeWay Press, 2007): This Bible study for guys and girls addresses all areas of purity.
- *For Parents Only: Getting Inside the Head of Your Kid* by Shaunti Feldhahn and Lisa Rice (Multnomah Books, 2007): This book enables parents to understand why their children do what they do.
- *Introduction to True Love Waits* by Jimmy Hester (LifeWay Press, 2004)
- *Sexual Resolutions* by Paul Kelly (LifeWay Press, 1999): Help students distinguish principles of Christian sexual behavior and modify their behavior to reflect those principles with this group study.
- *Living Pure Inside Out* by Bill Hughes (LifeWay Press, 2002): Helps students know how to stay pure while living in a sex-saturated world.
- *Student Survival Kit* by Ralph W. Neighbour Jr. (LifeWay Press, 2007): A resource to help new Christians explore important topics like sin, doubt, and sharing their faith as they walk with God.
- *The Search* by Robert S. McGee (a student version of *The Search for Significance*), LifeWay Press, 2004: Help students build their sense of self based on what God says about them with this Bible study.
- *Your Girl: A Bible Study for Mothers of Teens* by Vicki Courtney (LifeWay Press, 2006): Provides the tools to help mothers raise godly daughters in an anything-but-godly world.
- *www.education.com* (information on bullying)

7

OLDER YOUTH MARKERS

BY MIKE WAKEFIELD & PAM GIBBS

Adolescence—a time of change and development. You've got to be ready for it so you can help your teen get ready for it. Even then, the roller coaster will provide enough dips and drops and curves to make you want to quit.

But you really can't quit. You've got to help your teenager navigate through all the changes and guide him toward mature and responsible adulthood. On the path of purity, this may be the most challenging stretch you'll face. But it's incredibly important that you roll up your sleeves and stay at the job. More than ever, you've got to parent with the end in mind. If you persevere, the benefits will be more than you could ever imagine.

Purity Marker
DRIVER'S LICENSE

Emphasis: Balancing Freedom and Responsibility

1. Marker Description

Life changes forever when a teenager gets his driver's license. In some respects, this change is positive. Students can experience a new degree of freedom—which they desperately crave. On the other hand, that freedom opens the door to poor choices, especially in the area of purity. This marker in a student's life is an excellent opportunity to talk about the responsibilities your child must bear to maintain purity as he is increasingly away from your watchful eye and accountability.

As a parent, understand that at this time, your child...

- **Is experiencing more freedom than at any other point in his life.** He is making more decisions independently of a parent's influence.
- **Craves independence.** This desire for autonomy and freedom from parental involvement and input is a very normal and natural part of adolescent development. It is a necessary part of a teen growing into maturity. While this may feel like rejection to you as a parent, it is not you she is rejecting. She wants autonomy from authority, as evidenced by her rebellion against anyone in authority.
- **Will be expected to display more responsibility in many areas, including family chores (running errands), maintaining a part-time job, and transporting others.** He will also be responsible for displaying maturity and wisdom in decision-making. However, statistically speaking, your child will make mistakes (and possibly have a wreck) while driving.
- **Is beginning to experience a change in her relationship with you as a parent.** She may feel torn between trying to submit to your authority and leadership while at the same time trying to broaden her freedoms. Along the way, she will have numerous opportunities to learn from you and your experience or to use her freedom to move away from your family's core values (Prov. 22:6).

2. Your Teen Needs to Know...

- **The freedom of driving comes with greater responsibility.** He needs to understand the weight of responsibility of operating a vehicle and how he could harm others if he does not treat this responsibility seriously.
- **That she is still responsible for submitting to authority in various ways.** Your child is responsible for honoring traffic laws, including limits on cell phone usage and texting while driving. She also must honor laws about the number and age of passengers in the car.
- **You have entrusted her with a lot by letting her drive.** Your child has a responsibility to honor that trust by exercising care while driving and being honest about where she is going and what she is doing. She needs to know that you will hold her responsible for honoring that trust and that she will be the one who faces the consequences if that trust is betrayed.
- **New temptations come with this new privilege.** Where will he choose to go? Whom will he go out with? Will he honor your curfew? With the increased privileges come the increased temptations to misuse those privileges. Many teens make poor decisions as new drivers. They often say "yes" to every new temptation that comes their way because they were caught off-guard by it.
- **He needs new sources of accountability.** Since you can't be with your child at all times to help him make good decisions, your child needs to choose key friends and influences (like a mentor) who will hold him accountable and challenge him when he is on the cusp of making a poor choice. Strong, godly friends are a key point of accountability for teens.
- **Your child needs to establish strong boundaries concerning sexual activity.** Automobiles can lead to a great source of sexual temptation, especially if your child has not established physical boundaries that she will not cross.

DRIVER'S LICENSE

3. You Need to Know...

- **Letting go when a child begins to drive is a difficult experience for you as a parent, but it is necessary for your teen's emotional and social growth.** It represents one of the first release points for your teen as she begins to launch into adulthood. It is a great teaching and trusting opportunity for you as a family, even though you may be frightened by it. While your fear is understandable, it is important that you avoid the temptation of parenting out of that fear.
- **Make sure you set rules for driving.** Identify appropriate consequences and be consistent in following through on those rules. Some boundaries might include times when your child can

or cannot drive (on the weekends, after 10 p.m., only on side streets, etc.), who will pay for insurance and gas, and who else (especially friends and members of the opposite sex) will be allowed to drive or ride in the vehicle. Once you've set the guidelines, it's incredibly important for you to follow through with any negative consequences that might result from your child breaking one of the rules.

- **Your student is watching how you act behind the wheel.** This book has emphasized that you are always teaching your child. That truth extends to the roadways. What kind of example are you setting? Do you honor the speed limit like you expect him to honor it? Are you an overly aggressive driver? Do you drive after having a drink at a restaurant? Do you text while driving? Are you consistently distracted by other things? These can be touchy questions, but they serve as solid reminders that the rules of the road are often more caught than taught. Your teen will emulate your behavior, so be careful about the example you set.

4. Tips for Handling Young Drivers

- **Grant driving privileges in increments.** For example, when your child first gets her license, allow her to drive on back roads only. After a while, let her drive on main streets in your town. Then progress to minor highways and then major highways.
- **Create a driving covenant between you and your child.** In that covenant, set up responsibilities that he must live up to and identify the consequences for breaking any portion of the contract. Items within the contract might include car maintenance and repair, curfew time, and/or geographic distance he can travel. Keep in mind, though, that a covenant includes responsibilities on your part as well (such as providing insurance or praying for your teen before he drives to school).
- **Talk with your teen about the boundaries that she has set in regard to purity.** This includes physical purity (such as making out in the car), but is not limited to that. For example, you can talk about whether or not your child will see a movie containing sexual or lewd scenes or references (this guards emotional and mental purity). You may even want to write those down and post them on the refrigerator door or a bathroom mirror as a reminder. Remember that the biblical model for purity covers every area of life. Promoting that understanding is vital to making progress down the path of purity.
- **Continue to require "family time."** Even though your teen may demonstrate an outward disdain for anything connected with a

scheduled family time, you need to insist on setting aside times for the family to be together. Since he is experiencing new freedoms and wants new responsibility, you might try giving him the responsibility of planning the family time periodically. This allows him to speak into this time and to assert adult behavior.

DRIVER'S LICENSE

Purity Marker
DATING

Emphasis: Healthy Relationships with the Opposite Gender

1. Marker Description

Dating. The dreaded marker. Dad brings out the shotgun to polish in front of the fellow who has come to call on his daughter. Mom gets a little teary-eyed as she watches from the window as her "baby" leaves to pick up his date. From a child's perspective, this is the point at which teens begin to face in earnest the temptation to compromise their purity. Suddenly, the temptation is no longer theoretical; it is very real. How does a teenager have a healthy relationship with a person of the opposite gender in a way that doesn't compromise his commitment to purity?

As a parent, understand that at this time, your child...

- **Is starting to learn how to relate to the opposite gender** (Phil. 2:3-4; 1 Tim. 5:1-2). As your child moved through the markers of childhood, he noticed the obvious physical differences between the genders. As he grows older and begins to date, though, he begins to understand that the differences go far beyond just biological make-up. Your child is learning the stated rules (hold the door open for a girl) and the unspoken rules (don't ask a woman about her age or her weight; don't make fun of a guy in front of his buddies), as well as what the opposite gender needs and wants (love, respect, time, and so forth).
- **Is defining boundaries (emotional, physical, verbal) with the opposite gender** (Eph. 4:29; 1 Cor. 6:19; Prov. 4:23). Along with understanding how to relate to the opposite gender come boundaries. Your child is learning not only to define those boundaries for herself, but also how to respect and honor those boundaries with others. Teens who do not learn how to honor boundaries will experience difficulty in future relationships.

- **Will be facing pressure to start dating and to participate in activities modeled by their peers** (Rom. 12:1-2). Both genders face the pressure to date and find a girlfriend or boyfriend. Girls feel the pressure of being "chosen" by a guy. Guys feel pressure to maintain an image that may include the label of a "player." This pressure is compounded by the constant hassle from their peers to engage in sexual activity.
- **Will be facing pressure to act a certain way to appear appealing to the opposite gender.** Instead of living in and celebrating their God-ordained uniqueness (Ps. 139), teens often give in to what is expected of them. Dressing immodestly, sending inappropriate text messages, and engaging in inappropriate sexual acts or lewd conversations are all common pressures teens experience when they are looking for acceptance and approval from the opposite gender.

2. Your Teen Needs to Know...

- **Determining why she wants to date beforehand will save her a lot of grief.** Is your teen trying to build a meaningful relationship or simply trying to live up to an expectation set by peers and society? If she can begin dating for the right reasons, she can avoid the traps and temptations that often come in this phase of life.
- **Pretending doesn't pay off.** Rather than living some kind of lie, teach your child to be himself around girls instead of pretending to be something he's not. Of course, the same holds true for girls in their relationships with guys. In the end, both parties will be miserable if someone is pretending. But when you teach your child to build a relationship on honesty and trust, you are helping him establish a good foundation for future relationships.

DATING

- **Everything she hears isn't true.** Your child's peers may be telling her about stuff they are doing, but she needs to know that not every relationship is like that. Your teen needs to learn early that the idea of "everyone's doing it" is a lie, even if it seems that way at her school, on TV, or in the movies.
- **Treating a date with respect is important.** Your student should be careful to honor the other person's purity as well as his own. Remind your child to treat the other person the way he would want his future spouse to be treated. Just as important, your teen should not allow another person to treat him disrespectfully. He is worthy of respect no matter what he may have done in his past.
- **Accountability is easier when on a group date.** There are some benefits of group dating — accountability being one of the greatest.

When teens hang out together in the early stages of dating, they can call each other out on unacceptable behavior, including physical touch and activities (movies watched, where they hang out, etc.).

- **Look to older, godly couples to learn how to treat the opposite gender with honor and respect.** Older couples can be a valuable source of insight and wisdom. Watch how they treat each other. Ask questions about how they established and honored boundaries. Find out how they protect their purity, even if they are married.

3. You Need to Know...

- **Healthy dating involves a progression: group dating, double dating, solo dating.** Determine the age or level of maturity at which your child can move from one stage to the next. Before your child enters each stage, reinforce the importance of maintaining a pure heart, mind, and body. Also, provide opportunities for group dates or double dates.
- **The age at which your children begin to show interest in dating will vary.** Three siblings may begin group dating at three different ages, depending on maturity level and interest. Children who show little interest in dating early on need to be affirmed and not labeled as abnormal or odd. They may simply be drawn to other interests.
- **Don't let your own fears or personal history cloud your parenting.** Many parents live vicariously through their children. For example, a mother who wasn't considered pretty or popular by the guys may urge her daughter to dress or act a certain way to attract those popular guys. A father who struggled with his own sexuality may overreact to a son who shows little interest in girls. Instead, use this stage in your child's life as an opportunity to deal with your own emotional baggage and allow God to heal any wounded area still showing itself in your life.

4. Tips for Dating Discussions

- **Discuss healthy boundaries (physical, emotional, verbal) with your teen.** This really needs to be a "team effort" between you and your teen. You can answer questions like, *Is it OK to hold hands? Kiss? What about giving your heart away too soon? What is OK to say or do in front of a girl or guy?* Help your child think through the reasons behind those boundaries, as well as the consequences for violating them. He needs to know that boundaries are meant for his protection and safety, not just a way for you to control him.
- **Discuss the "rules" your family has established for dating.** Is a potential date required to come over to your house before you will

allow your child to go out with him or her? What activities are off-limits? *(Examples: R-rated movies, being alone in a bedroom together, texting after a certain time at night)* As you lay out the rules, explain the reasons behind these boundaries so your child understands your reasoning — even if he disagrees.

- **Help your teen explore her individual, unique, God-given personality.** Affirm the gifts you see in her. Provide opportunities for her to develop her skills (take a class, join a club, etc.). Encourage girls and guys to avoid altering, compromising, suppressing, or changing that uniqueness for another person. You may even want to use this time as an opportunity to talk about times you compromised your God-given design for the sake of acceptance — as well as the consequences you endured for doing so. Honesty and vulnerability in this area can go a long way in gaining your teen's respect and trust.
- **Set an example of honoring the opposite gender at home.** The simple act of saying "thank you" and "you're welcome" can communicate volumes. Don't talk badly about your spouse in front of your children. Affirm the importance of both genders as a reflection of God's image. Use teachable moments (TV shows, movie clips, song lyrics) to talk about discrimination against genders and/or respect for the opposite gender.

DATING

Purity Marker
EXCLUSIVELY DATING

Emphasis: Defining Boundaries and Commitment

1. Marker Description

When teenagers begin dating exclusively and spending more time together, the likelihood of sexual activity increases. The dynamics of the relationship, combined with normal aspects of adolescent physical development, might make it more difficult for a teenager to make wise decisions. Since the temptation is greater, teens need to develop and rely upon a firm commitment to purity. You can help them with their commitment by providing strong accountability coupled with strong boundaries.

As a parent, understand that at this time, your child...

* **Is developing a stronger ability to make commitments.** In previous years, "going out" consisted of saying that you were boyfriend and girlfriend and then completely avoiding each other in person! Dating relationships in middle school are typically transient and short-term in nature. However, as your teen begins to mature, he develops the capacity to make and keep a commitment to a person.
* **Is moving into more serious relationships, making an exclusive commitment to one person.** While you may understand the temporary nature of teen dating, your teen may take the relationship very seriously. Any attempt to minimize the relationship or her feelings toward a significant other will be met with strong resistance.
* **Is facing new, stronger temptations in regard to sexual activity.** Teens confuse their feelings of attraction with true love (1 Cor. 6:13-20; 1 Thess. 4:1-8). Many teens feel very strongly about their boyfriends or girlfriends and cannot distinguish this puppy love from a biblical, long-lasting, committed relationship.
* **May be more likely to compromise her faith values in favor of a dating relationship** (2 Cor. 6:14). Missionary dating becomes

commonplace. Many teens think they can change the other person or pull him up spiritually. In all likelihood, a relationship is only as strong as its weakest partner. Many committed believers find themselves in compromising situations that challenge not only their sexual purity but also their spiritual growth and personal holiness.

- **Has a greater opportunity to be an example to younger students in the area of nurturing dating relationships** (1 Tim. 4:12). As your teen matures, he has the chance to impact those in younger grades by setting an example of purity. Younger teens need to know that purity is possible, even in today's culture. Older teens have the opportunity to demonstrate that teenagers are capable of living pure lives.

2. Your Teen Needs to Know...

- **Exclusive dating is an opportune time to renew a commitment to sexual purity.** If your teen has broken that commitment in the past or has not made a commitment to purity at all, this is an important time to pledge before God and others that he is seeking God's best for himself and for others by pursuing purity.
- **How to evaluate and reaffirm godly standards for dating.** Before now, your student's standards for dating basically have been theoretical since she wasn't all that involved in the dating scene. Now, those standards move from principles on paper to principles to live by. Before she commits to dating exclusively, help her evaluate whether or not that guy meets the standards for dating.

  Your student should ask questions such as: *Is he or she a believer?*, *Does he or she draw me away from God?*, *Am I becoming a better person because he or she challenges me?* Part of this reflective process should be a time when she evaluates expectations and standards for her future spouse. If a prospective date doesn't meet those expectations, she should seriously reevaluate the relationship. Unfortunately, teens often reject the standards in order to keep the relationship rather than ending the relationship in order to keep the standards.

- **Increased temptation is a reality to be recognized.** As a teen grows in a relationship with another person, strong feelings can lead to great temptation to act on those feelings. And sometimes, physical desire and emotional attachment can become intertwined, making it more difficult to resist the temptations that seem so natural.
- **How to equip himself to remain pure during this time.** Help your teen set limits on the amount of time alone he will spend with a date. Set limits on the types of physical affection shown (holding

EXCLUSIVELY DATING

hands, kissing, and so forth). Help your child stick to the established curfew and teach him not to spend time in places that he knows will be tempting (parties, alone in the car, and so forth).

- **Why he or she should keep the feelings about teen relationships in proper perspective.** The here-and-now feels like the only thing that exists to someone in her teens. Feelings seem strong, real, and eternal. But the truth is that very few high school couples go on to marry. While dating in high school provides helpful experience for relating to the opposite gender, it is not the only thing that deserves your teen's focus during this stage of life.

- **How to develop a biblical understanding of the true meaning of love.** Our culture places low value on selfless, self-sacrificial love. Instead, it equates love with sexual expression that satisfies selfish desires as its ultimate pursuit. This time in a teen's life gives him the opportunity to understand what God really wants for him in relationships and to understand what true love really looks like.

3. You Need to Know...

- **You are still an active part of your teen's accountability strategy.** While your teen desperately wants independence, this increasing freedom does not negate your parental responsibility to hold your teen accountable. Taking the approach that, "He's going to do whatever he wants anyway" provides no safety net or safeguards that could protect him from a lot of heartache. It is important for you to keep the lines of communication open so you can encourage and hold him accountable.

- **The sexual temptation faced by students in this time sharpens dramatically.** One girl put it succinctly when she said, "It's not whether or not we'll have sex, but when." Teens face strong temptation from several fronts — their own hormones and desires, the wants and wishes of their significant other, and the pressure to conform to a subculture that glorifies sexual expression in any form. You need to provide support against that tide.

- **Teens need to define the characteristics of a godly spouse.** As a parent, you play a major role in helping your teen understand that dating just for the sake of status or to avoid loneliness is a weak foundation for a relationship. You can take this marker as an opportunity to help her process in her heart and mind the characteristics she wants in a future mate and to pursue only those relationships that bear the fruit of that character.

4. Tips for Exclusive Dating

- **Encourage your teen to follow through on commitments.** Many teens become so connected (obsessed) with a boyfriend or girlfriend that they fail to follow through on commitments to sports, academics, church, and volunteer work. Watch for signs of this happening and follow through on those hard conversations about balance and perspective in relationships.

- **Set limits on the amount of time your teen can spend with a significant other.** You must determine how much of your teen's free time can be spent with a date. Find answers to things like, *Are they allowed to go out on both Friday and Saturday nights? How often are they allowed to send text messages? When is the boyfriend/ girlfriend allowed to come over to the house?* These are all questions that you will need to address.

- **Look for signs of abusive or unhealthy relationships.** Teens often mistake the signs of abuse for signs of true love and concern, especially if your child struggles with self-esteem and wanting to feel needed and wanted. A victim can be male or female. Take action if you see any of the following occurring in your child's relationship:
  - ▸ Checking up on the other person by calling or driving by
  - ▸ Calling the other person names, even in jest
  - ▸ Teasing the other person in a hurtful way (publicly or privately)
  - ▸ Acting jealous of the other person's friends, family, or coworkers
  - ▸ Reading the other person's e-mail, texts, or other private matters
  - ▸ Demanding to know where the other person is at all times
  - ▸ Threatening to harm the other person (or self) if the relationship ends
  - ▸ Trying to control what the other person does and says

EXCLUSIVELY DATING

Purity Marker

PROM/BANQUET/ FORMAL

Emphasis: *Wise Decisions*

1. Marker Description

Prom night. It's the stuff that teen dreams are made of. Elegant dresses. Updos. Tuxedos. Limos. Fancy country clubs. And in some cases, the hotel room. At this special time, many teens make poor decisions either deliberately or in the heat of the moment. Many teens (especially girls) regard this as a "coming out" of sorts in which they try to dress and act more mature than they actually are. They want to act out in adult behavior that matches their adult dress.

As a parent, understand that at this time, your child...

- **Views prom/banquet/formal as the culmination of a relationship.** Many couples that have been dating exclusively for awhile see themselves as a couple in love. They symbolize this commitment to each other during this prom season by engaging in sex (some for the first time), moving the intensity of the relationship beyond what is good and healthy (Song of Sol. 2:7; 3:5; 8:4).
- **May be encouraged to spend an "all-nighter" away from home, often alone with the opposite gender for the first time.** After-prom parties are common and often take place without the sanction or support of school administration or parents. These can take place in a variety of locations — hotels, country farms, a popular hangout, or even a student's home. You and your child will need to decide whether or not these parties are safe and positive places to be.
- **Needs to make wise decisions before the event so that he is not faced with these choices in the heat of the moment** (Prov. 15:22; 19:2; 20:18). Very rarely do teens (or adults) choose wisely when they are wrapped up in the glory and joy of the moment. Creating a plan and strategy ahead of time can reduce the risk of poor choices when the pressure is on.

2. Your Teen Needs to Know...

- **That it's OK to lower her expectations for the event.** This moment is a big one, but help her keep it in proper perspective. Remind her that there will be many other occasions when she will have the opportunity to dress elegantly, go out to a fancy restaurant, and enjoy the company of a significant other. Help her to avoid putting too much value on this event so she won't be tempted to make a decision she will regret later.

- **How to set boundaries ahead of time so he can make wise decisions on the night of the event.** As mentioned earlier, your student doesn't need to wait until he gets to the after-prom party to decide how to handle situations. In many situations, a teenager will make the wrong decision if it's made in the heat of the moment.

- **The value of going to this event with a group of friends.** There is safety in numbers. Keep in mind, though, that this safety is only as strong as the accountability he has with the other members of the group. There is no safety in numbers if everyone is bent on engaging in dangerous or unwise behavior.

- **This is an opportunity to model discernment, discretion, and purity.** It doesn't take much courage to just say you're waiting until marriage to give your body and heart to someone else. It doesn't take character to skip an outdoor after-prom keg party when it's raining. It doesn't take confidence to turn down a prom date when you know the evening won't turn out well. The prom/banquet/formal season gives your student the chance to stand up for her worldview, to demonstrate the confidence that comes from knowing that a single night doesn't define her worth or popularity. It gives her a chance to exhibit maturity by avoiding situations that will lead to nothing but heartache and bad consequences.

PROM/
BANQUET/
FORMAL

- **What his plan of action will be ahead of time.** This is one step where you will play an active role — in developing a plan and providing an escape route for bad situations. *What should your son do if he gets in over his head or finds himself in a tempting situation? Whom will your daughter call if she doesn't have a safe ride home? What if the prom becomes a source of temptation? What is his way out if he's tempted to lust or treat another person without respect?* Sit down with your student (and encourage him to sit down with his date) to talk through these issues beforehand. Let him know that you are willing to do whatever he needs you to do to help him protect his purity.

3. You Need to Know...

- **What boundaries you will set for this event.** What will be your role in the event? Will you chaperone? Will you allow this to be an all-night event for your teenager? When will curfew be? Will you provide an alternative event at your home after the event? When discussing these boundaries, your teen needs to know that these boundaries are being set for safety, not for control.
- **Prom/formal/banquet is a big deal to most students.** Many teenagers see this as the highlight of their high school careers. As a parent, you will need to exercise wisdom in determining when your teen is old enough to attend (many schools allow underclassmen to go with a student in a higher grade) and how much money and time you are willing to invest. And your teenager may have trouble keeping the event in perspective, so you will need to provide that voice of reason, even if that perspective is unpopular.
- **Many limos come stocked with alcohol.** Before your son or daughter gets into a limousine, make sure the alcohol (and the resulting temptation) has been removed.
- **There are lots of resources on the Internet that will help you do prom on a limited budget.** Do an online search of "prom tips for parents," and you'll be amazed at what resources, tips, ideas, and support you'll find for this season in your child's life.

4. Tips for the Big Event

- **Take a stand on modesty, especially if you have a daughter.** Don't believe the lie that it's impossible to find anything modest. It is possible to find an attractive—and even glamorous—dress that doesn't reveal everything. However, you may be forced to endure many trips to many stores over many weekends to find one. That means you'll need to plan ahead when you begin to hear the rumblings of prom talk. If you shop early, you are more likely to find something that both you and your daughter like. You may even want to plan a girls' weekend to another city (that has more shopping choices) and make it a special event for both of you.
- **Offer a "no questions asked" policy for picking up your teen at any point in the evening.** Your child needs to know that you will be there for him, even if it means picking him up in a questionable place and not asking a bunch of questions if he is too flustered (or drunk or embarrassed) to talk at that moment. Once the night is over (the next morning or over the course of the weekend), you can calmly

talk about what happened. Use this as a learning experience and a teachable moment in your teen's life (and possibly your own).

- **Emphasize guidelines for proper behavior toward members of the opposite sex.** Reinforce earlier discussions about respect and honor. Review some of the simple actions that demonstrate respect: holding the door open, allowing the other person to order dinner first, saying "thank you," staying away from lewd conversations and comments. Respect and honor are not often valued among teenagers. Challenge your teenager to act against the norm by demonstrating that he values the other person.

- **Discuss the importance of making wise decisions and the consequences of making poor decisions.** Try the following exercise as a discussion starter: Ask your child what she wants to be doing 10 years from now, and then five years from now. Then ask her, on a scale of 1 to 10 (with 10 being the most important), how important are those plans? What could happen at prom that might derail those plans? This will help your child understand that even a momentary lapse of reason and judgment could have huge ramifications for the future. A look at the long-range scope of life will give added perspective that most teens lack.

- **Communicate with other parents.** Find out what they are doing for their children during this time. Ask about the boundaries they have set up for the night (curfew, where their teenager can go and with whom, and so forth) Inquire about after-prom parties. If you are willing, work together to provide a fun alternative to the student-organized post-prom drinking fest. Knowing what other parents are doing is a huge advantage for you.

PROM/
BANQUET/
FORMAL

- **Communicate with the school system.** Find out the rules regarding dress, activities, chaperones, and unacceptable behavior. Find out if there are any safeguards, such as random alcohol searches, metal detectors, and other preventive measures that will ensure a successful night. Also find out the consequences for not following the school's policies on prom night. Discuss these policies with your teen.

HIGH SCHOOL GRADUATION

Emphasis: *New Challenges*

1. Marker Description

Throughout high school, a teenager generally has operated under the authority of her parents. For nearly two decades, she has been taught to respect and obey the values established by her parents. And that's good because that's how God planned it (Ex. 20:12; Deut. 6:6-9; Eph. 6:1-3). However, high school graduation should represent a shift toward freedom for the teen and "letting go" for the parents. With this marker, teens begin identifying and living by their own personal core values, including their personal beliefs about purity, in every aspect of life. Once those values have been identified, teens must determine how they will integrate those values into daily life.

As a parent, understand that at this time, your child...

- ◆ **Has cause to celebrate what has been accomplished.** Reaching this marker is no small task and will serve as a marker for the rest of his life. Its importance cannot be minimized and deserves a special degree of recognition (Josh. 4:1-9).
- ◆ **Understands that new challenges are part of her immediate future.** The process of closing one chapter of a teen's life means special focus must be given to the new chapter about to begin. The transition from life as a high school student to life after high school will likely be the most challenging adjustment in a teen's experience to this point (Phil. 3:12-14; Heb. 12:1-2).
- ◆ **Will be experiencing a wide range of emotions.** You may have already noticed these mood swings. Many teens are excited about graduating. But they may also feel restless, like they've outgrown high school and youth group. They feel sad as they experience the "lasts" (last home football game, last prom, etc.). They may be scared, especially if they

have been in a small, insulated environment and are moving to a much larger, less safe place like a university. They want independence but sense an impending change in their relationship with you as a parent. They fear the loss of the relationships they now have (friends, boyfriends, and so forth) and are nervous about establishing new relationships in the future.

2. Your Graduate Needs to Know...

- **This stage is a beginning, not an end.** While one stage of life is being fulfilled, a stage providing greater freedom and requiring greater responsibility is about to begin in earnest. While it is normal to feel anxiety about the unknown, your young adult needs to know that this change can give him a fresh start and a new challenge. It can spur him on to greater maturity and stronger character.

- **What she believes and why.** This marker gives your young adult the opportunity to examine personal beliefs and determine how those core values will define her boundaries and behavior. She must answer the question, *How will my faith (and what I believe about purity) influence my daily life?* In the very near future, she will have the opportunity to make choices without your influence or accountability. She will have the chance to make her faith personal or reject it all together. And as she moves into adulthood, she will be responsible for defending and acting on those beliefs. She will need to think through questions such as: *How will my life (behavior, decision-making, boundaries, and so forth) after high school be different than my life during high school? How will it be the same?*

- **He can make a difference in the world around him.** Hopefully your child has been able to identify and develop his gifts and skills and can feel some confidence in how God has wired him for life and service. As your child grows older, he should seek more opportunities to use his gifts and abilities to make a difference in the lives of those around him. This could happen through missions work, voluntary community service, or any number of other avenues. One key to maintaining holistic purity is learning to invest in the lives of others, putting their needs and desires above his own.

HIGH SCHOOL GRADUATION

3. You Need to Know...

- **You are your child's role model of freedom and responsibility.** She needs to see how you emphasize the power of personal purity in every aspect of your life. *What television shows do you watch? How* *do you treat your spouse? What off-color jokes do you tell?* These all demonstrate your understanding of a pure lifestyle. You have the freedom to behave how you want, and your student notices how you live out that freedom.

- **It is normal for your child to act like a grown-up one minute and then act immaturely the next.** Hopefully, over the course of his senior year, there have been fewer wild fluctuations between childish and adult behavior. While it is easy to expect high school graduates to act with maturity all the time, the reality is that they are still figuring it all out. Don't expect perfection.
- **It is normal for your child to want more independence, and it is important for you to grant it in incremental stages.** The more you let your teen experience freedom while still under your watchful care, the more you can help by intervening if she makes mistakes or misuses that freedom.
- **It is important to emphasize the role of the church in life after high school.** When your child graduates from high school and possibly moves away for college, work, or the military, he will have the freedom to choose whether or not to get involved with a local church. While your child is still at home, use this marker to communicate the value, benefits, and responsibility of being a part of the body of Christ. Help your teen understand the overarching importance of being with God's people rather than telling him that it's just a good thing.

4. Tips for Guiding a Grad

- **Provide appropriate levels of freedom, while emphasizing responsibility and the need for accountability.** For example, many parents allow their high school seniors to choose (within limits) their church attendance. You may insist that the family worship together on Sunday but make attendance an option on Wednesday night. You can use this freedom to discuss the reasons behind his choice to attend or not, as well as the things he will miss by not being there. You could also let your teen have a later curfew, but with the responsibility of communicating where he will be that evening. If curfew is broken, enforce a consequence of an earlier curfew.
- **Continue the process of letting go, shifting your role from teacher to counselor or advisor.** This may be a difficult transition since you've spent the last 18 years trying to instruct and lead your child. This will require you to be quiet when she makes a mistake. It will mean

that you let her make mistakes and suffer the consequences. It will probably be tough on you, but it is healthy. It prevents you from becoming a "helicopter parent" and builds the confidence your teen will need to leave the nest and get on with her life.

- **Find ways to celebrate the accomplishments of your teen.** This could include a special ceremony that honors your teen while pointing her toward the demands and expectations of the future. You can look online for rite of passage resources that will give you some ideas for how to do this. For example, you could invite the adults who are significant in your child's life to come to a special party and share a significant piece of wisdom or give a token that symbolizes that wisdom. These adults could pray over her, asking God to instill wisdom in her life. The event could conclude with dinner or snacks.
- **Help your teen find resources that will help him maintain his purity beyond graduation.** When you visit colleges, research the collegiate student ministries there. Find out how incoming freshman can get involved. Get a list of local churches in the area. Find out which ones have strong college ministries. You may even find out if a college offers a freshman mentoring program that will offer some additional accountability.

HIGH SCHOOL
GRADUATION

Helpful Resources
FOR OLDER
YOUTH MARKERS

The experiences of older youth represent steps toward adulthood. Their activities tend to balance greater freedoms with greater responsibilities. While they can feel the insecurity of childhood at times, they are determined to embrace the independence of life on their own. You still have a role to fulfill under the guidelines of Deuteronomy 6. Here are some resources—some geared toward parents and some toward teenagers—that may help you on this part of the path of purity.

- *Living with Teenagers* magazine: This monthly magazine offers practical answers to real-life questions from a Christian perspective to help parents develop a growing relationship with teens.
- *Revolutionary Purity* by James Jackson (LifeWay Press, 2006): This study encourages students to commit to purity and become actively involved in living it out in their families and throughout the world.
- *Essential Gear: Your Guide to Life After High School* (LifeWay Press, 2005): Practical help for graduating seniors, including reference information such as a world religions chart, tips for buying a car, and so forth.
- *Heart Connex* online devotions, *www.heartconnex.com:* Designed for the busy family, these free, 20-minute Bible study devotions come via e-mail and are designed to involve both students and parents.
- *When True Love Doesn't Wait* by D. Tony Rankin and Richard Ross (LifeWay Press, 1998): This booklet can help teenagers who are desperately seeking forgiveness in the area of purity.
- *True Love Waits Takes a Look at Courting, Dating, and Hanging Out* by David Payne (LifeWay Press, 2000): This study emphasizes the importance of defined courtship and dating principles.
- *Becoming a Man* by Robert Lewis (LifeWay Press, 2006): A DVD-based study for fathers and their teenage sons to develop a realistic, God-centered view of manhood.
- *Confident* by Carol Sallee (LifeWay Press, 2009): This book teaches girls to walk in daring confidence, not because of anything the world has to offer, but because of Christ's indwelling presence.
- *True Princess* by Erin Davis (LifeWay Press, 2010): This Bible study will help girls understand the importance of living as a daughter of the the King.

YOUNG ADULT MARKERS

BY MIKE WAKEFIELD & PAM GIBBS

From those first wobbly steps across the living room, arms outstretched toward you, to the confident steps across the platform to grab a diploma, your child has come a long way in what might seem to be a very short time. But whether time has flown or crept by, your relationship with him is changing. The time has come for you to let go and let him fly.

While that's obviously easier said than done, it is a vital part of leading your child toward independence—and toward the next phase on the path of purity. But even though your child is now a young adult and things are still changing, one thing remains the same—it's still your responsibility to move him toward spiritual transformation. And you still have much to offer as he continues his journey down his own personal path of purity.

Purity Marker
COLLEGE

Emphasis: *Maintaining Standards*

1. Marker Description

Sending our children off to college is bittersweet for most of us. We are excited about the new opportunities that await them, and we are proud of the things they have achieved that have led to this next step in life. But it's also gut-wrenching to send them out into the world. It's hard enough just to let them go, but it's even more difficult when we know what they will be facing on this section of the path of purity. We can't really be close at hand to see and hear what they are experiencing anymore. We have to entrust them to God and pray that they will hold fast to the values we have worked hard to instill in them.

As a parent, understand that at this time, your child...

- **Will be spreading his wings.** What an exciting time for your child as a new chapter in his life is beginning. He will probably experience a wide range of emotions between the joy of a new journey and the heartache of leaving home.
- **Is anticipating a sense of freedom she has never had before.** Many of the rules your child has lived under and abided by are seemingly gone. At least the constant accountability that your presence brings will be gone from her life.
- **Will be encountering different worldviews.** Your child may have encountered some different worldviews in high school, but that level of exposure will be nothing like what he will encounter when he sets foot on a college campus. His beliefs will probably be tested, along with his commitment to purity.
- **May be more vulnerable to sexual temptation.** Your child will likely encounter lower purity standards among her peers. Plus, an atmosphere of sexual freedom pervades some college campuses. This, along with her newfound freedom, could make her susceptible to temptation.

- **Will start making decisions on his or her own.** Allowing your child to make decisions on his own is a good thing. That's what you have equipped him to do. However, it is a little scary to watch him do it. You need to continue providing input, wisdom, and lots of prayer; but you have to allow him to make the choices.

2. Your Young Adult Needs to Know...

- **Sexual intimacy outside of marriage has consequences.** Remind your child that the consequences of sex outside of marriage remain the same, even though he will probably know of many students who engage in sexual activity.
- **Not everyone is doing it.** Though it may seem like most—if not everyone—around her is sexually active, that's not the case. Plenty of students have also chosen to remain sexually pure. Remind her of the story of Elijah in 1 Kings 19. He thought he was alone, but God reminded him of all the others who had remained pure.
- **It's important to maintain purity standards.** The temptation to lower his standards of purity may be great, but you should continue encouraging your child to maintain the godly standards he has set.
- **It's important to maintain spiritual disciplines.** Now is not the time to become lax on the spiritual disciplines of Bible study and prayer. Remind your child that straying from a consistent walk with Christ will open a weak place in his spiritual armor. Share your own spiritual struggles or triumphs from this phase of your life.
- **Keep the lines of communication open.** Encourage your child to talk to you about what she is experiencing. Remind her that you are on her team and she can always call home.
- **The friends you choose make a huge difference.** The Scripture says, "Bad company corrupts good morals" (1 Cor. 15:33). Your young adult needs to be very discerning about selecting friends because college friends have a tremendous influence on the present and the future.

COLLEGE

- **A lot of people meet their future spouse in college.** That doesn't mean your child should go on a spouse hunt, but it does mean she should wisely consider the kind of people she dates. She needs to make sure those individuals are on the same page with her when it comes to a relationship with Christ and a commitment to purity—just in case the relationship develops into something more.

3. You Need to Know...

- **Your college student needs you to let him go... to a point.** Even if your young adult is in college, letting go will probably be difficult. The desire to hang on will be strong, but you need to cut him loose. It's time for him to step out on his own. You don't want to be a helicopter parent—hovering over your child, making every decision for him, solving every problem, and providing for every need. That part of your work is done. You can remain available to offer advice and support, but he needs to start feeling the weight of adult responsibility.

- **Expect changes.** Your child is going to change. She will leave as one person and come back a different one. Don't worry. It happens to all who leave home. Some of the changes will make you smile, while some will be cause for concern. It's OK to point out these areas and talk about the changes your young adult is experiencing. In fact, this may help both you and your child to process the changes. And you will change too. Family dynamics will shift for every family member. Being open to your child's perspective on how you have changed will help her be open to the changes you see in her.

- **Your student is still looking for your help in setting boundaries.** Though your young adult has new freedom and is making decisions on his own, your job is not over. He will still look to you for guidance. Instead of just telling him what to do, walk together through what he is facing and help him discover the right choices.

- **Your young adult will be challenged.** There are many challenges facing your child as she leaves for college, especially in the realm of purity. She could be challenged about her faith, values, and commitment to sexual abstinence. Be ready to walk with her through this time.

- **You might start becoming smart again.** You probably went through a time when your child considered you the dumbest person on the planet. However, as he starts moving into the world and facing grown-up things, you'll suddenly become smarter in his eyes. You may have a greater voice of influence than you have enjoyed in a while, especially as he gets into later college years.

4. Tips for College...

- **Celebrate.** This time is a big deal! Though your heart may not feel like celebrating, make this a joyous time as your young adult starts a new chapter. Find ways to celebrate before he goes to college, such as a special family trip or an overnight trip with just the two of you. Host a party for your child and his friends before he leaves.

- **Review values and standards.** Before your child leaves, find time for a refresher conversation about the purity values she has set and the commitment to purity she has made. Point out that her values and commitment will probably be challenged by what she sees, hears, and experiences at college. Remind her of your trust and your constant love and prayers, regardless of what the future holds.
- **Continue holding your child accountable to his purity commitment.** Don't be afraid to ask hard questions about what your child is experiencing at college. Encourage him to be honest with you. Talk about the challenges he is experiencing in relation to his values and commitment to the path of purity.
- **Encourage your child in his spiritual journey.** The statistics are alarming concerning what happens when Christian kids go off to college. Many of them drop out of church and become stagnant in their walk with Christ. Hold your young adult accountable for his spiritual walk. Encourage him to get involved in a local church and a Christian group on campus like Baptist Collegiate Ministry. Check out *www.sbccampusconnect.net*. This site allows you to give the name of your child to the Baptist Collegiate Ministry director at a specific university. The BCM director can then share your child's name with Baptist churches in the area that have college groups. If your child is not Baptist, the BCM director can help point him to other churches or Christian groups on campus.
- **Listen.** Be a good listener. Your child may need a place to unload and process all that is going on and changing in her world. Listen without condemnation or a need to comment about everything.
- **Don't be shocked at what you hear.** If you're going to give permission for him to tell you all, don't be shocked at what he shares about life on campus. Listen to the stories and help him remain true to the godly values and biblical standards you have instilled.
- **Pray.** You may find yourself praying for your child more than ever before, especially since she is out of your sight and out of your nest. Pray that your young adult will...
  - ▸ Follow hard after Christ
  - ▸ Find Christian friends
  - ▸ Hold to established values and boundaries
  - ▸ Be discerning
  - ▸ Make good decisions
  - ▸ Be a bold witness and a person of influence for good

Purity Marker
SINGLENESS

Emphasis: *Embracing Every Stage of Life*

1. Marker Description

Maintaining purity while single is an uphill battle in the midst of today's hedonistic culture. Among the more than 5,000 ads the average person sees per day, the blatantly amoral worldview in the media, and the experiences of their colleagues and coworkers, today's single person must navigate the lonely waters of purity with little support from those around them. That is why it is so critical for parents and for the church to come alongside singles to challenge and encourage them.

As a parent, understand that at this time, your child...

- **Is facing the marriage of friends around them.** A single adult deals with a variety of emotions as his or her friends are paired off in matrimony. Excitement, jealousy, and fear are common struggles that singles must face.
- **May be struggling with self-esteem.** With many of their friends marrying, some singles ask this poignant and honest question, *Why not me?* They may question what's wrong with them if they aren't being asked out, aren't finding that special someone, and are left alone on the weekends. Many wrestle with a feeling that they have somehow been cursed or doomed because of some fault of their own. In the midst of this struggle to find acceptance and worth, many singles begin compromising their standards of purity, as well as their commitment to a godly relationship. They "settle" because they think there is no other option.
- **May be wrestling with loneliness.** Singles often battle feelings of loneliness. In their attempt to find companionship, love, and satisfaction, they may be tempted to forsake their sexual purity. They think that giving into this temptation is the only solution to

loneliness. With no end to solitary life in sight, many singles adopt an apathetic attitude toward purity. To them, finding a shallow imitation of intimacy is better than living with an empty feeling.

- **May be perfectly content in his marital status.** Many adults are purposely delaying marriage and family. These young adults see other priorities (education, financial stability, career development) as more important than marriage and family.

2. Your Child Needs to Know...

- **Being single can be a rich and rewarding time of life.** Your child needs to know that life doesn't begin with an "I do" at the altar. He needs to know that whatever his state of life, God is leading him and has big plans and dreams for him right now — not just somewhere in the future when he settles down. God works in singles and can do amazing things through them.

- **Maintaining purity is possible.** However, many singles listen to the lies of culture about a person's rights to do whatever they want to meet their needs. They listen to the voices of their peers who seem to lead happy, fulfilling lives apart from purity. They allow Satan to lead them astray and into bondage that looks like freedom. Your child needs encouragement to remember that purity is possible.

- **Accountability is critical.** Maintaining purity as a single adult in today's culture is a minefield of temptations, conflicting ideologies, and desires. Having others who will walk this journey with her, holding her accountable, encouraging her, and giving her wise counsel when needed is critical. Your child needs to know that trying to go it alone when it comes to keeping a commitment to purity is a scary and dangerous road to walk.

3. You Need to Know...

- **Your young adult probably doesn't think you understand what he's going through.** In his eyes, you are older, and you are not alone. You do not have the same needs as he does. You can't possibly be tempted by sins of a sexual nature. Whether or not these assumptions are correct, your child probably thinks you cannot relate to what he is experiencing as a single person. Because of that, he may be hesitant to talk about the struggles of being single in a couple's world.

SINGLENESS

- **Your "jokes" about marital status hurt and can cause heartache.** While you simply may be trying to make a connection, add a little humor, or help her feel better, it doesn't work. For some single adults, constant reminders that they are alone only adds to their frustration, confusion, fear, and loneliness. The solution is to lay off the jokes. Just don't go there.

- **Family functions and get-togethers can be difficult.** Think about it. A family reunion consists of families with children, all talking about their families and their children. What could be a more miserable place for a person with no spouse and no children? Add to that the sweet, clueless aunt who tries to set her up with that person who is "perfect" or the grandmother who talks about her dying wish to see your young adult get married. It's a lot for one person to handle, even in the healthiest of families. For a single person, family functions can be just another reminder that they don't fit anywhere — not with married friends and not with family members who are dealing with their own family issues.

4. Tips for Parenting Singles

- **Celebrate and encourage your child's pursuits.** If he wants to pursue advanced degrees, support his effort. If she's unsure about college and wants to just enter the work force or join the military, pray and talk through the decision with her. If he wants to be a missionary overseas for several years following college, offer financial support if possible. If your single finds passion in mentoring students rather than pursuing a family of his own right now, encourage that. Ask questions. Show that you are interested in and care about what your child cares about. Most importantly, don't exert any undo pressure or question motivations. Remember that God is ultimately in control of your child's life. Trust Him to lead him in the right direction.

- **Don't always focus on other family members who have spouses and children.** It is understandable that you would dote on your grandchildren. And it's natural that you might relate better to children who have spouses because you share that common element. However, your single adult needs to know that she matters as much to you as a married sibling. Don't always talk to her about what the grandkids are doing. Don't make your other children the focus of your conversation. Your single adult wants to know what is going on in others' lives, but she also wants you to know — and appreciate — what is going on in her life.

- **Refrain from asking "So, are you dating anybody yet?"** A single person gets tired of hearing that all the time. It reinforces the myth that single people are incomplete. If he isn't dating but wants to, it is a painful reminder of what he longs for but doesn't have. When your child is ready for you to know about a significant other, he will tell you. Until then, don't ask. Just leave that subject alone. This would include any helpful hints about online dating services or charming members of your church's singles ministry.

- **Encourage her to take risks, try new things, and pursue activities that would be impossible or impractical as a married person or a parent.** Studying abroad, international mission trips, advanced education, adventure weekend getaways, and serving in the church can all be enriching and rewarding experiences that would be more difficult for someone with a spouse (and family).

SINGLENESS

Purity Marker
ENGAGEMENT

Emphasis: *Preparing for the Future*

1. Marker Description

As a person commits to be with another for the rest of his life, purity is heavy on his mind. The commitment to sexual purity with the future mate becomes more difficult. Many view engagement as "basically married," leading to several justifications for premarital sex. Purity of the mind also poses a special challenge as one's thoughts drift toward the anticipation of intimacy in a marriage relationship. Ironically, at this time, the person is able to maintain a private lifestyle, free from the discipline of parents. Accountability is crucial.

As a parent, understand that at this time, your young adult...

- **Is making one of the biggest commitments of his life.** Outside of a relationship with Jesus, choosing a spouse is the biggest decision in life, one that should not be made without prayer and wisdom.
- **Faces temptation with the future mate (premarital sex) or alone (pornography, masturbation)** (1 Cor. 6:18-20; 1 Thess. 4:3-5). Temptation takes on a different form when an engaged couple must deal with desires that naturally grow within the context of a relationship. An engaged couple naturally wants to express their love to each other in a physical manner and must deal with the temptations to short circuit the God-ordained plan to wait until after the marriage ceremony.
- **May be facing the consequences and/or forgiveness of a sexual history, either of her own or her mate's** (Col. 3:12-14). As a couple begins the process of becoming one in marriage, they must deal with past infidelity and talk through how they will address issues related to sexuality that surface because of each person's history (sexual activity, abuse, poor parenting).

- **Is desiring a life with one partner of the opposite sex** (Prov. 18:22; 2 Cor. 6:14; Gen. 2:24). Finding one's life partner is an amazing discovery, filled with strong emotions of joy, apprehension, fear, remorse, confusion, and elation. Be prepared for your young adult to display a wide variety of emotions (even conflicting emotions) as he prepares for marriage.

2. Your Child Needs to Know...

- **Past actions can carry consequences for the future.** Every impure thought, word, and action from a person's past and present have an impact on the future — not only for your child, but also his mate. Part of becoming one in marriage is handling the impact of one's actions on the other person. Therefore, in marriage, one must think of his spouse and not solely of himself. Your young adult will need to talk with his future spouse about how past actions will affect the marriage. For example, if one person has been sexually active, both partners must understand the possibility of a sexually transmitted disease. The couple must deal with the emotional baggage of past relationships and may need to work with a counselor if there has been a history of sexual abuse.
- **Marriage is a commitment before God that starts with engagement.** Your child needs to discuss her commitment to purity with her future spouse to be sure they are both in agreement. It is tempting to act on sexual desires because they'll be getting married soon anyway. Allowing that rationalization is a dangerous temptation. Your child will need to determine what safeguards to keep in place to remain pure during engagement.
- **How important it is to find a close friend or spiritual leader to hold him accountable for thoughts and actions.** At this stage, your child may be tempted to forsake accountability in favor of privacy, but privacy can be a doorway to indiscretion. If he will remain open to accountability, he is protecting his future marriage and future spouse. Understanding that accountability guards your marriage and spouse makes one more likely to be honest and truthful with those significant mentors who care about that relationship.
- **How important it is to find a godly, stable married couple to serve as mentors.** Even before the wedding, your young adult and her future spouse should spend time with a couple who share their experiences in an honest and loving way. They need to be able to observe how these marriage veterans behave toward each other and ask questions

about how they maintain purity within their marriage. They should discuss the struggles they have faced and overcome and any fears or questions related to marriage. Being vulnerable and honest with another couple will help not only with accountability, but also with cultivating those characteristics in your child's marriage.

- **Why she should discuss purity expectations with the future spouse.** Purity is something to be guarded in marriage, not just as a single person. Your child needs to talk with her future spouse to make sure they are both in agreement on how to guard purity in the marriage relationship. What movies will be allowed into the home? Will they use computer software to weed out pornographic or questionable materials? Will either of them ride in a car alone with a person of the opposite gender? Issues like these must be addressed.
- **The wedding ceremony should be an expression of continued commitment to purity.** The commitment your child and his spouse make on their wedding day is not expressed in remaining sexually abstinent but remaining faithful to one person for life.

3. You Need to Know

- **Your child may still have lots of questions about sex.** With sexual intimacy looming on the horizon, many single adults have questions: *What is it really like?*; *Is it like what is described in the media?*; *What if I am not appealing to my spouse?*; *Will it be painful?*; and *How can I "get ready," if that's even possible?* While the prospect of talking to your adult child about sexual issues may leave you feeling very uncomfortable, you can play a pivotal role in helping him develop a healthy attitude and correct understanding of sex.
- **If your daughter (or future daughter-in-law) chooses oral contraception as a form of birth control, she will likely begin taking this medication several months prior to the wedding as prescribed by her doctor.** This does not mean that she and her future husband are sexually active. Do not panic and do not assume that anything inappropriate is happening.
- **The wedding is not about you or your family.** This special event should focus on the love between your child and her spouse. You can be of valuable help to your child by communicating to family and friends that you support the couple's decisions related to the ceremony, wedding party, reception, guests, and other elements. If a family member or friend is offended by something, don't try to fix it by making your child do something to please others. Family and

friends should address their own issues. It's not your responsibility, and it's not your child's either.

- **Your child needs to plan the details of the wedding.** It is not your responsibility. You can offer to help (and many children welcome the help), but do not take over. If you do, the wedding becomes what you want instead of what your child wants. Stepping back into an advisory role shows that you have confidence in your child's decisions. It also forces your child to become independent and more self-sufficient and mature.

4. Tips for the Days Before the Wedding

- **Share your purity story with your child.** If the story is a positive one, reinforce the benefits and rewards of remaining pure. If your story involves mistakes and lapses in purity, point out the consequences and why purity matters.
- **Be vulnerable and willing to answer questions about your marriage.** Your child needs to know the real story of sexual intimacy: that it is nothing like what is portrayed in Hollywood. Guide him to understand that sexual intimacy is about giving, being selfless, understanding each other's needs, and being willing to meet those needs. Explain that sexual intimacy is a process of learning about each other—not just a physical act to release pent-up hormones.
- **Encourage the couple to discuss their sexual expectations with each other, as well as their boundaries for a pure sexual relationship in marriage.** While you cannot force your child to talk to her future spouse, you can certainly encourage them and applaud their efforts to build their marriage on a strong foundation of truth and communication.
- **Encourage premarital counseling.** Many churches and pastors require couples to undergo premarital counseling before they will allow the wedding to take place in that church. If there is a history of abuse for either partner in the marriage, encourage counseling for that as well. Keep in mind that a couple's finances are sometimes limited, so if appropriate, you might want to offer to pay for the counseling as a wedding gift.

ENGAGEMENT

Purity Marker
MARRIAGE

Emphasis: Covenant Relationship

1. Marker Description

At this stage in your child's life, you take another step back. Your role is one of consultant or adviser—when called upon. The last part of that statement is very important. There may be moments when you have to bite your tongue as you watch your young adult and her new spouse navigate their way through the first few years of marriage. Hopefully the character you have helped build in your child will carry her through some of the rocky moments of marriage. The purity lessons you have shared will help her remain committed to the person God has chosen for her.

As a parent, understand that at this time, your child...

- **Is excited about the life ahead with her mate.** No one gets married hoping the relationship ends in a divorce. Everyone starts with a sense of excitement and anticipation about the life ahead. That's the way it should be.
- **May be coming to grips with the reality of marriage.** At some point in the first few days, weeks, or months, the honeymoon really will be over. There will be an argument or disagreement, and ugly things will be said. It happens in the best of marriages. The reality of life lived with another person sets in. It's not all going to be chocolate and roses. Marriage takes work.
- **Will be busy learning all the nuances of his spouse.** We are all quirky, and part of marriage is learning all the quirks of your spouse. No matter how well your child thinks he knows the person he's marrying, he will still deal with some unexpected stuff that will rise to the surface once they start living together in marriage.
- **Has started the process of tackling real life.** It's beginning to sink in that your young adult is just that—an adult. Together with her spouse, your child is learning how to make grown-up decisions with grown-up consequences.

2. Your Young Adult Needs to Know...

- **Marriage is designed and ordained by God.** Marriage is not the world's idea; it's God's. He designed marriage relationships for His purpose and glory. This is important to remember since it emphasizes the sacred nature of the commitment and can encourage husbands and wives to work at making the marriage work when it seems easier to quit.
- **Marriage is more than a commitment.** It is a covenant between a man, a woman, and God (Gen. 2:18,21-24).
  - ▸ *A covenant marriage is serious.* The Hebrew word for covenant (*berith*) relates to a cutting of the flesh that draws blood. That's pretty serious! In the Old Testament, covenants were so serious that God held those who broke them accountable.
  - ▸ *A covenant marriage is sacred.* In the Bible, a covenant was the most serious, sacred, and solemn agreement that could be made between human beings. It is sacred to enter into a covenant marriage before God, family, and friends.
  - ▸ *A covenant marriage is sacrificial.* There is no such thing as covenant without sacrifice, and marriage is designed to be the most sacrificial of all relationships. The Bible says husbands are called to love their wives as Jesus loved the church and that wives are called to submit to their husbands in love (Eph. 5:22-25). A covenant represents total surrender from both sides.
- **It's not too late to commit to a life of purity.** Even if your young adult was not sexually pure at the time of the wedding, he needs to make a new commitment to remain faithful to his spouse and to remain sexually pure for the rest of his life.
- **The grass is never really greener.** When marriage gets hard—and it will get hard—the commitment to faithfulness and purity cannot be tossed aside. In fact, the commitment can serve as the glue that holds your child accountable for her actions. It also helps to remind your young adult that no temporary pleasure can improve upon the joy and security that comes from intimacy within a committed marriage relationship.
- **Determine ahead of time to make wise decisions.** Choose to avoid compromise in any relationship. Encourage your young adult to set standards that would not put him in compromising situations, such as not riding alone in the car with someone of the opposite gender who's not his spouse.
- **There is help and encouragement in surrounding your marriage with Christian couples who are committed to purity in marriage.** Godly Christian couples can be great models for a young marriage. They

MARRIAGE

can also be a source of wisdom and guidance in many areas in a marriage, especially the difficult ones.

- **Be aware that there is more to remaining pure than just staying away from a physical affair.** There are other ways a husband or wife can derail a purity commitment. A pornography addiction is one such problem. We usually think of this as just a man's problem, but women can struggle with this also.

- **Unreal expectations can cause resentment.** Your young adult and her spouse need to have clear communication when it comes to their sexual relationship. If one of them — or both of them — hold unreal and/or unmet expectations, this could cause resentment and put their purity at risk.

3. You Need to Know...

- **Your affirmation of the marriage is important.** You probably have lots of feelings about the marriage of your young adult. Hopefully, most of those feelings are positive. Regardless of your feelings, though, you need to be affirming of this union and committed to helping them be as successful as possible.

- **Your role is shifting toward modeling and mentoring.** You have been and remain the No. 1 example of what a marriage relationship should be like. At times you will need to take a mentoring role in the marriage. Just be cautious about stepping in to offer guidance. Follow the lead of your child and his spouse. If they ask for your help, gladly step in. If you see areas where they could use some guidance, carefully and gently give your help. There is a fine line here between helping and meddling. Just be cautious and prayerful. And understand there are exceptions to all this.

- **Discussions about sexual intimacy may be uncomfortable, but necessary.** These conversations may be rare, but be prepared to guide your newly married child. Many young adults enter marriage with the overly glamorized view of sex that is promoted by the media. This can lead to unrealistic and unmet expectations, which can lead to resentment and other problems in the marriage. Be prepared to help your young adult understand the real version of sexual intimacy.

4. What You Need to Do...

- **Model purity and faithfulness.** Continue to set the example for purity. That is the greatest wedding present you could ever provide — and it's a gift that keeps on giving over time.

- **Renew your commitment to purity.** Perhaps this is a good time for you and your spouse to renew your commitment to faithfulness and purity. This can be done privately between just the two of you, or you could involve other members of your family to further your example of a lifetime of purity and as a means of holding you both accountable to the commitment.
- **Pray.** You know marriage involves hard work. You know what it feels like once the newness wears off and the stresses of life begin to hit close to home. You may even know the pain of failure in marriage. Paul told the Corinthians that God allows us to experience things so we can minister to those who are experiencing the same struggles (2 Cor. 1:3-4). Part of your ministry to your child and her spouse is to pray for them as they begin the work of marriage and start their own journey down the path of purity.

MARRIAGE

Helpful Resources
FOR YOUNG
ADULT MARKERS

In a sense, one of your goals as a parent is to work yourself out of a job. As your child moves out of adolescence and into adulthood, you want him to display maturity and integrity. You want him to be responsible and live out a commitment to purity in every area of his life. But the truth is that you never stop being a parent. Your roles may change, but you still have commitments and responsibilities as the primary spiritual developer of your child—even if that child is grown up. Here are some resources that can help.

- *Collegiate*: In-depth Bible studies, relevant articles and features, editorials, and reviews of music, film, and books can all be found in this college resource that has the look of a magazine.
- *The Love Dare* by Stephen Kendrick and Alex Kendrick (B&H, 2008): A 40-day guided devotional experience that will lead your heart back to truly loving your spouse while learning more about the design, nature, and source of true love.
- *The Five Love Languages* by Gary Chapman (There are several versions of this resource, including one for single adults.) This study helps you identify your personal love language and then also the love language of others.
- *Men Are Like Waffles, Women Are Like Spaghetti* by Bill and Pam Farrel (Harvest House, 2007): Humorous yet insightful, this book shows couples how to delight in their differences and enrich their relationships. It teaches husbands and wives how to bring out the best in each other in ways God intended—with acceptance, service, encouragement, forgiveness, devotion, motivation, and edification.
- Festivals of Marriage: At these conferences sponsored by LifeWay Christian Resources, you can leave the busyness of life behind and retreat to a place where your only responsibility is to focus on your husband or wife, your marriage, and your relationship with God.

9

PURITY DETOURS

BY MIKE WAKEFIELD & PAM GIBBS

Wouldn't it be great if we had a moral GPS to guide our decisions and actions? Whenever a questionable situation popped up, we could just program the GPS to lead us out of trouble. We'd never stray from God's plan, and we'd save ourselves a lot of heartache along the way... as long as we followed the instructions we were given.

But God did give us a way to stay on course through His Word. And, all too often, we ignore the Bible's guidance and go our own way. The truth is, none of us are righteous on our own (Rom. 3:10), and we all fall short of God's design (Rom. 3:23). Our natures want to drive us off the path of purity and into some dangerous detours that can hinder our walk with God and create chaos in our lives.

That's why it's important to recognize the potential pitfalls and to do all we can to avoid them.

Defining the concept
OF PURITY DETOURS

In May 2010, a series of storms dumped record amounts of rainfall on Nashville, Tennessee, and its surrounding areas. For the better part of two days, the rains came down—and the floods came up. Roads were swamped. Property was destroyed. Individuals were stranded. Some even died.

Even those residents who didn't suffer any physical or property damage from the rising waters had to adjust to a new life—albeit temporarily. Because many of the roads in town were flooded, commuters had to find new ways to get to familiar places. They had to take detours, which often slowed them down or left them confused.

Detours have a tendency to do that. They usually take more time than normal because detours steer you off the normal route. Often, we find ourselves out of place and out of sorts. Whenever possible, staying on the main road is best.

Spiritual Sidetracks

As aggravating as traffic detours can be, the most dangerous detours we face in life have nothing to do with backroads or highways. But they have everything to do with the spiritual path we walk—the path of purity.

Of course, that's not really a new insight. It's not hard to look back on our lives and see where we've been sidetracked in one way or another. From the very beginning, God has had a plan, and Satan has been working hard to undermine that plan by drawing humans away from the life God wants them to lead.

In Genesis 2, God placed Adam in a marvelous garden with one simple rule: Don't eat from one tree (vv. 16-17). Everything else was fair game. But that one tree would lead to trouble. So what happened? You know the answer. Satan slipped in and started planting seeds of doubt. He implied that God was somehow holding out on His prized creation by restricting their access to the tree (3:4-5). He also made the prohibited object look more desirable than it really was (3:6-7).

In the end, Satan got just what he wanted. Humanity took its first spiritual detour and found itself separated from God by sin. And we've been taking spiritual detours ever since.

Purity Detours

When the True Love Waits team began discussing the concept for this book, we got very excited about the idea of life markers. We immediately saw the benefit of helping parents lead their families toward purity by highlighting significant life events.

But it wasn't long before we realized that the markers were only part of the story when it comes to the path of purity. We had to acknowledge that every path has spots where it could be very easy to leave the right road and stray into dangerous areas. We knew we had to address those detours as part of our overall plan for ministering to parents.

Jimmy Hester provided a quick look at the six detours in chapter 3. In this chapter, Mike Wakefield and Pam Gibbs have gone deeper into each one: abuse, sexual activity, pregnancy and abortion, pornography, homosexuality, and living together.

It is not our intention to scare you or to assume your child is stuck on one (or more) of these detours. But we do want you to understand they are very real. Satan is still trying to convince humans that God is holding out and that what we've been told to avoid is really sweeter than what we have. And he's using the detours to make that happen in many situations.

The best way for you and your children to live an abundant life is to stay on the path of purity. If we can help you avoid these detours, this chapter will have been worth the effort.

ABUSE

1. Detour Description

Unfortunately, abuse is common in today's world. Abuse can strike anyone at any age and can take many forms. Physical violence. Verbal attack. Sexual exploitation. Emotional neglect and abuse. All of these can cause scars that influence future relationships, especially romantic relationships. Hopefully, your child will be spared the heartache of abuse, but statistically, he will likely become the victim of some sort of abuse at some time in his life. The extent of the abuse and its effects will vary, but as a parent you need to be aware of the signs of abuse. Armed with information, you will be more prepared to help your child heal and thrive beyond the pain inflicted upon him. Left without any help, he may struggle to establish a healthy marital relationship one day.

2. Types of Abuse

- **Verbal abuse:** This type of abuse uses words and language to harm another's spirit or hamper personal development and autonomy. This type of abuse includes but is not limited to: put downs, name-calling, blaming, threatening to leave the relationship, ignoring, disrespecting, humiliating, or criticizing consistently. This type of abuse is dangerous because it's not easily recognized. Many people play off this verbal abuse by saying, "It's just a joke."

- **Emotional abuse:** This abuse is often tied to or accompanied by other forms of abuse. It can include rejection, humiliation, isolation (not allowed to go outside of the house, being locked in a room alone for long periods, and so forth), and terror (putting a loaded gun to a child's head, threatening to kill family members, and so forth). Many times, the abuser will use phrases such as "you tempted me" or "you asked for it" (i.e., sexual assault).

- **Physical abuse:** This is defined by the use of physical pain or the threat of pain to intimidate or harm another person. Physical abuse has taken place even if bruising or similar physical evidence does not occur. Forms of physical abuse can include punching, kicking, slapping, burning, and cutting, along with other forms of violence.
- **Sexual violence and abuse:** This abuse involves any unwanted sexual contact, including rape, date rape, molestation, incest, being forced to engage in certain sexual activities without explicit consent, being called by a derogatory sexual name (example: being called a "ho"), and unwanted sexual remarks.

3. Signs of Abuse
- **Verbal:**
  - negative self-image
  - self-destructive acts
  - delayed emotional development
  - antisocial behavior (difficulty making friends)
  - extreme behavior — either extremely compliant or aggressive
- **Emotional:**
  - feelings of shame
  - behaving older or younger than his age
  - depression
  - anxiety
  - substance or drug abuse
  - extreme dependence on others
  - emotional instability
  - constant phone calls, texts, or e-mails from another person
  - being called derogatory names or being put down
  - name calling or putting another person down
- **Physical:**
  - unusual and unexplained bruising
  - constantly saying she was clumsy
  - not wanting to dress around others
  - shies away from touch
  - flinches at sudden movements
  - fearful in the presence of adults
  - wears inappropriate clothing (long-sleeved shirts or pants on a summer day)
  - destructive toward self or others

ABUSE

- **Sexual:**
  - difficulty sitting or walking
  - displays knowledge of sexual acts beyond their appropriate age
  - avoids a person excessively
  - doesn't want to change clothes in front of others
  - sudden acquisition of money, clothes, or gifts without an explanation
  - sexually transmitted disease, especially in children younger than 14
  - sudden change in appetite
  - consistent complaint of unexplained physical problems

4. Tips for Helping Your Child Through This Time

- **Communicate that the abuse was not his or her fault.** Many people who are abused try to deal with the situation by blaming themselves:
  - "I asked for it."
  - "I should have known better."
  - "If I had just done what she asked..."
  - "I deserved it."
  - "I am such a bad person."

  Your child needs to know that no one deserves abuse. No one brings it on themselves, and it is never justified. This kind of support may be more difficult for you to offer if the abuser is a friend or relative. However, it is absolutely critical that you communicate that the abuse was not the child's fault.

- **Believe your child.** Your child needs someone in her corner. Even if you question aspects of the incident or if the event even happened, something is going on with your child that has led her to report the abuse to you. You must work with your child, authorities, and appropriate professionals (social workers, psychologists, doctors) to work through this problem. Act as if the incident is true. Do not discount what your child says. It is better to "over-respond" than to avoid responding at all.

- **Report the event to proper authorities.** In some states, adults (including parents) are held legally liable if they do not report suspected instances of abuse to the police. Regardless of the legal liabilities, you discount the incident and discount the abused child if you choose not to report the event. In your child's eyes, your refusal to do anything shows that you don't care about what happened, that you care more about the abuser than the child, or that you don't believe your child. There is no shame in reporting abuse. There is nothing to be gained by "keeping it in the family." Nothing positive, helpful, or healing happens when you ignore the cries of a child (whatever his age) who reports abuse.

• **Get counseling—even for the whole family.** The impact of abuse shakes the entire family system. You and your family could benefit greatly by the expertise of a godly, trained counselor who can help you find healing in the midst of a painful experience. As the parent, you play a major role in setting the stage for healing. By being proactive with counseling, you demonstrate a concern for your child and a willingness to do whatever it takes for him to find peace and to help him work through the emotional ramifications of the abuse.

ABUSE

Purity Detour
SEXUAL ACTIVITY

1. Detour Description

Some teens and young adults are involved in sexual activity and see nothing wrong with it. In fact, some who sign True Love Waits pledges feel this way. They equate the pledge to sexual purity before marriage as just a pledge not to have intercourse. They deem other sexual activity—like mutual masturbation and oral sex—as OK. And this is not just a problem among older teens and young adults, but younger teens as well.

2. Reasons Your Child May Take This Detour

- **They have desires.** Teens' hormones are raging. They are now physically capable of sexual activity and want to try it out.
- **Lots of stimulation.** Even for those who try, shutting out all the sexual messages in our sex-saturated society is virtually impossible. The temptation to be sexually active can be found in anything they watch, listen to, and read. They can't even drive down the road without sex being used to sell something on a billboard.
- **Wrong messages.** The messages they receive from our society about sexual activity are that everyone is doing it, it's cool, and there are no consequences. Since teenagers are physically primed and ready, the messages seem to give them permission to explore their sexuality.
- **Pressure.** Even the most committed and godly teen can feel the pressure to be sexually active. Whether it's from the guys in the locker room or the girls at the sleepover, there is pressure to "do it." As noted, we could even say that society itself puts pressure on teens to be sexually active.
- **A need for love.** There is a longing in every teen's heart to be loved. Unfortunately, this emotional longing is not filled in the right way for too many teenagers. They don't receive the intimacy they crave in their homes, so they try to substitute a sexual

encounter for that missing intimacy. For example, a young lady who has never experienced proper love, affection, and security from her father may try to fulfill that longing through physical relationships with guys.

3. Avoiding the Detour

♦ **What your child can do...**

▶ *Don't be fooled by wrong messages.* Your child needs to be discerning when it comes to the messages he is receiving. Help him know that what the media and some peers may be telling him about sexuality is not necessarily the truth.

▶ *Stay away from temptation.* The best way your child can resist temptation is to avoid putting herself in a position where her standards could be compromised. She should set standards such as not being alone with someone of the opposite gender, not watching R-rated movies or any movies or shows with nudity or sexual situations, and so forth.

▶ *Set clear standards now, not in the situation.* Your child can't wait to set his standards until the temptation occurs. Set them now. If he waits, the emotions and physical desire in the heat of the moment will make it very difficult to resist the temptation.

▶ *Stay spiritually consistent.* Your child needs to stay focused on her ongoing relationship with Christ. Encourage her to take the time to read and study the Scripture passages concerning sexuality (1 Thess. 4:1-7; 1 Cor. 6:15-20) and to memorize Scripture that will help her successfully battle temptation (Ps. 119:9-11; 1 Cor. 10:13).

▶ *Keep the end in sight.* Your child lives in an instant gratification society where we want what we want, and we want it now. She needs to choose delayed gratification when it comes to sex. If she wants to present herself pure to her spouse, she can't compromise now.

▶ *Understand the consequences.* Your child needs to know there are physical, emotional, and spiritual consequences to sex outside of marriage. Help him not just give the consequences a passing glance, but understand the devastation that can be caused through premarital sexual activity.

♦ **What you can do...**

▶ *Help your child set clear purity standards.* Talk with your teen about the godly standards he needs to set. Study the Scripture

SEXUAL
ACTIVITY

together to understand the biblical guidelines. Make sure your child understands the broad definition of sexual activity and that any sexual activity before marriage is wrong. You might even take the time to write out the standards with your teen, then both of you could sign the document and post it in your child's room.

▶ *Encourage your child to make a True Love Waits commitment.* When your student ministry or church provides this opportunity, encourage your child to participate. Mark this important commitment with a visual reminder such as a ring or necklace. Follow up your child's commitment with support and accountability. If your church is not providing a TLW commitment time, take the lead in talking with other parents about planning one. If nothing else, provide a time for your child to make this commitment in the privacy of your home.

▶ *Provide safe environments.* Your child will want to spend time with friends of the opposite gender. She will likely have romantic interests in the midst of these relationships. Provide opportunities for your child to interact with her friends in a protected setting. For example, open your home for your child and her friends to hang out together. Supervise outings. And involve other parents to help you.

▶ *Set godly standards for media.* Help monitor the sexual messages your child receives by setting appropriate standards for what your family will and will not watch. You can also help your teen's discernment by watching things together and discussing a program's meaning and message and how it lines up against biblical standards.

▶ *Model purity.* Live out the adage "More is caught than taught." You are setting the example for your child concerning purity. Don't send mixed messages. Model a pure life by what you watch, listen to, and read. Your child is also picking up on your speech and noticing the way you treat your spouse. Seek to be pure in all things.

▶ *Pray.* Pray that your child will not be led into temptation. Pray that when he does face temptation, he will remember Scripture and biblical guidelines concerning sex. Pray that he would be bold and strong, able to stand up against the pressure to be sexually active. Pray that he would value his purity and the purity of his friends.

4. Getting Back on Track

If your child is already sexually active, here are some ways to help her get back on the right track.

- **Confront but don't condemn.** You have to confront the issue, but speak the truth in love.
- **Revisit biblical standards.** Discuss the standards that were set before, the reasons for setting them, and how you can help your child follow these in the future.
- **Discuss reasons for activity.** Talk about why your child feels the need to be involved sexually.
- **Talk about starting over.** Help your child know that it's not too late to start over. Some teens feel that since they have gone a certain distance sexually, they might as well go all the way. Or if they have lost their virginity, they feel they might as well keep having sex. Remind your child that God's design for sex is still real and that she can receive His love and forgiveness if she will confess her sins and repent.
- **Encourage godly activity.** Sometimes it's a matter of what your child is committed to. If he is spending his time helping others or engaged in some form of personal spiritual development, the tendency to be sexually active may be less tempting.
- **Reestablish your support.** Remind your child that you are on her team. Tell her that you love and support her and want to encourage her as she strives for purity.
- **Maintain an attitude of grace and forgiveness.** We all mess up. We all need grace and forgiveness. Keep that in mind when you deal with a child who has strayed.

SEXUAL
ACTIVITY

PREGNANCY & ABORTION

1. Detour Description

There are several "nightmare" situations that most parents hope they never have to face. One of those is hearing the word "pregnant" from your unmarried child.

Here are some alarming and sobering statistics:

- In 2006, 750,000 women younger than 20 became pregnant. Overall, 71.5 pregnancies per 1,000 that year occurred among women aged 15 to 19. The rate declined 41 percent from its peak in 1990 to a low of 69.5 per 1,000 women in 2005. However, for the first time since the early 1990s, overall teen pregnancy rates increased in 2006, rising 3 percent.[1]
- There were 200,420 abortions among 15 to 19-year-olds in 2006, meaning that 27 percent of pregnancies among 15 to 19-year-olds that year ended in abortion.[2]

These statistics are alarming, but can feel sterile. We can read them and feel sorry for those teens and their families but not be moved because it really doesn't affect us. In fact, we can sometimes pass judgment by thinking or saying something like, "Well, if their parents would have just..." or "How could anyone ever abort a baby?" or "They could have..."

But when it comes home, when it's your daughter or son, all of your feelings change. All your objectivity about teen pregnancy and abortion disappears because now it's *your* problem, affecting *your* family.

It's not a situation any of us wishes for, but it continues to happen to all kinds of families.

2. Reasons Your Child Might Take This Detour

- **Pregnancy**
  - *False sense of no consequences.* You already know that your child receives many, many messages about sex. However, very few of those messages, if any, deal with the consequences of sex before marriage. Most of the messages glamorize sex and portray teen sex in a positive light. If no one else is providing the truth, your child can easily get the false impression that nothing bad can happen when he has sex.
  - *Search for love.* Many girls who get pregnant do so because they are looking for someone to love them. That's the reason they have sex in the first place. They equate sex with love. If a guy is kissing them, touching them, wanting them, then he must love them. Much of this need a young lady feels is in correlation with the relationship, or lack of relationship, she has or had with her father. Some girls intentionally try to get pregnant because they think a baby will give them the unconditional love they are seeking.
  - *It can't happen to me.* Your child may think that pregnancy happens to other teenagers, but not to her. Even if she is using protection while being sexually active, it can still happen. Except for abstinence, every form of birth control has its flaws.
- **Abortion**
  - *No other choice.* Some teens view abortion as the only choice they have. Out of despair and desperation in what seems to be a hopeless situation, they turn to abortion to solve the problem.
  - *Easy way out.* Some teens know there are other options but see an abortion as the easiest solution. They don't want their lives to change, and they see abortion as a swift, easy answer.
  - *Fear.* Being pregnant is a terrifying experience for most unwed teens. They are afraid of being found out, afraid of what their parents will say or do, afraid of how a baby will change their lives, and so forth. Out of this fear, they believe an abortion will make it all go away.
  - *Pressure.* Some girls choose abortions because they are pressured to have one. The pressure can come from several directions, including the father of the baby or well-meaning, but misguided, adults. Pressure can also be applied by parents who, for whatever reason, feel abortion is the best answer.
  - *Financial reasons.* Some teens realize they can't financially support a newborn, so they see aborting the baby as the best solution.

PREGNANCY & ABORTION

3. Avoiding the Detour

+ What your child can do...
  - ▶ *Stay true to her purity commitment.* While this seems to be a "duh!" step to avoiding this detour, your child needs the simple reminder that as long as she stays sexually pure, she won't have to worry about this detour.
  - ▶ *Understand the realities of pregnancy.* Some teens have a romanticized version of what pregnancy is all about. Your child may need a frank discussion about the life-changing circumstances an unwanted pregnancy brings.
  - ▶ *Don't play with fire.* Some teens want to push the purity limit. They are the ones who ask the question, "How far is too far?" The truth is, if you go to the edge of the cliff, you're at great risk of falling off. Don't mess around sexually.
  - ▶ *Keep the long-term goal in sight.* Teens have dreams of what they want their lives to be. Help your child see how an unwanted pregnancy will derail those dreams.
+ **What you can do...**
  - ▶ *Hold your child accountable to her commitment.* Keep in mind that making a True Love Waits commitment is a huge step in remaining pure. However, the commitment must be backed up with support and accountability from you. Continue to remind her of the commitment she made and discuss struggles she may be having.
  - ▶ *Stay informed and aware.* Don't stick your head in the sand and blindly trust your child to stay sexually pure. At the same time, don't be paranoid. Ask questions. Keep the purity conversation going. It will be much easier to talk about purity if it is a frequent part of your conversations. Pray for a discerning heart to sense the struggles in your child's life.
  - ▶ *Help your child set clear boundaries for dating relationships.* Give your child input on what are and what are not appropriate actions and activities for your child and the person she is dating.
  - ▶ *Pray for your child.* Pray that your child would stay true to his purity commitment. Pray he would learn how to make wise choices. Pray that he will choose to date people who share his convictions about sexual purity. Pray he will continue to talk with you about any struggles he is facing.

4. Getting Back on Track

- **Step back and take a breath.** When you discover your daughter is pregnant or that your son has gotten a girl pregnant, you're probably going to experience a deluge of strong emotions, including anger, shock, disappointment, and grief. That's normal. Just don't respond to the situation out of those emotions. Take a step back and breathe. Pray for clarity and wisdom to know how to proceed.

- **Offer support, not condemnation.** In no way are we saying that getting pregnant outside of marriage is right. It's not. However, at this point what your child needs is your love and support. He needs to know that you still love and support him.

- **Talk through options and give guidance.** A decision will have to be made: keep the baby or put the baby up for adoption. Help your teen understand the options and what is entailed with each option. Assure your teen of your support regardless of the decision.

- **Maintain an attitude of grace and forgiveness.** There will probably be many moments that you want to lash out in anger and frustration at different people involved. Pray for the strength to maintain a calm attitude and to handle the situation redemptively.

- **Know that there is no easy solution.** Some may see abortion as an easy solution. But there is nothing easy about it physically, emotionally, or spiritually. Help your child do what's right, not just what seems easy.

- **Remember that God is sovereign.** Keep in mind that God is still in charge of this seemingly chaotic and devastating situation. He is able to bring something beautiful out of it for His purpose and His glory.

If your daughter has an abortion…

In the majority of states, a minor must have parental consent for an abortion. However, that's not true in all states, nor is consent needed once your daughter reaches 18. If she has an abortion without your knowledge or consent, many of the things listed above will apply. Most importantly, if she has confessed having an abortion to you, continue to love and support her. Also be ready to help your child deal with the repercussions of that decision, which may mean helping provide pastoral or professional counseling.

1. Kost K, Henshaw S, and Carlin L; Guttmacher Institute, *U.S. Teenage Pregnancies, Births and Abortions: National and State Trends and Trends by Race and Ethnicity,* 2010, 2, 6. Available from the Internet: *www.guttmacher.org/pubs/USTPtrends.pdf.*
2. Ibid., 7.

PREGNANCY
& ABORTION

Purity Detour
PORNOGRAPHY

1. Detour Description

While pornography is nothing new, the prevalence of the issue in contemporary culture may be greater than at any other time. Teenagers are entering puberty earlier. In addition, the avenues for accessing pornography have increased through the Internet and other technology, such as sexting.

While a relatively new topic in the discussion of purity, sexting continues to be a problem for teenagers. If you're unfamiliar with this term, sexting is the sending and receiving of sexual words and/or images, including nude and semi-nude pictures, by cell phone. According to a report by the National Campaign to Prevent Teen and Unplanned Pregnancy, 20 percent of teens have sent nude or semi-nude photos of themselves to someone else, and 39 percent have sent sexually suggestive messages.[1] Along with the emotional and spiritual damage of sexting, it also carries possible legal consequences.

Whatever form it takes, pornography can create a powerful addiction, attacking both the mind and the body. It creates confusion about the true meaning of love and the rightful place of sex. It clouds issues of self-esteem/body image and devalues others for the sake of physical pleasure.

What's more, pornography is not just a guys' problem. Studies reveal that roughly two-thirds of young men and one-half of young women agreed that viewing pornography is acceptable, whereas nearly 9 out of 10 (87 percent) young men and nearly a third (31 percent) of young women reported using pornography.[2] It is a detour from the path of purity that can affect both your son and your daughter—if it hasn't already.

2. Reasons Your Child Might Take This Detour

- **He is curious.** Although our society leaves little to the imagination, there is still enough mystery about sex that it stirs a curiosity in a teen to want to know more.

- **She lives in an over-sexed society.** You can't turn on the TV or even drive down the highway without being exposed to sex. It's used to sell everything from soap to hamburgers. This kind of atmosphere coupled with a hormone-charged teen is a bad combination.
- **He has easy access.** It used to be that unless your friend's dad had some "girlie" magazines hidden away, pornography was not that accessible. But that's not the case anymore. Porn is available at the click of a button.
- **She has desires.** As hormones rage, teens are looking for a way to satisfy their desires. Pornography seems to be an easy answer.

3. Avoiding the Detour

- **What your child can do...**
  - ▸ *Recognize the power of pornography and develop a plan to deal with temptation.* Your child needs to know that pornography is wrong and can lead to a destructive addiction. Talk about how to deal with the temptation to view pornography.
  - ▸ *Affirm a biblical view of sexuality, including issues of gender identity and showing proper respect for others.* Your child needs to know that in your home, you adhere to biblical values and expect him to as well.
  - ▸ *Set personal standards for media and technology use that will protect her body, emotions, and mind.* It's not too early for a young teen to set these standards.
  - ▸ *Establish accountability relationships with significant adults and other peers to add deeper levels of protection against pornography.* You should be your child's first level of accountability. But who else can serve in that role?
- **What you can do...**
  - ▸ *Stay up-to-date with culture and trends that could lead to your child's exposure to pornography.* Understand the dangers of pornography and its impact on both males and females.
  - ▸ *Work with your child to identify and set proper boundaries regarding technology and media use.* For example, place computers in high-traffic areas, limit time on the Internet, use Internet filters, and regularly review the history of sites visited on computers. Discuss the type of movies and shows that are appropriate for your child to watch.
  - ▸ *Teach your child the importance of purity in every aspect of life.* Discuss what it means to have a pure mind and how to

PORNOGRAPHY

maintain that purity. Talk about having pure speech and how important it is to talk properly to and about someone of the opposite gender. Sexual purity is very important, but God calls for His people to be holy in every aspect of life.

▶ *Discuss the destructive nature of pornography and possible consequences.* Talk about how pornography devalues others and sends the wrong messages about relationships. Help your child think about the future and how an addiction to pornography could have a negative influence on dating relationships and even marriages.

▶ *Model purity and integrity in every area of your life.* It's not OK to place limits on what your teenager can view when you routinely cross those boundaries yourself. Living a double standard is hypocritical, but it also erodes your effectiveness at speaking into the life of your child. To avoid this possibility, evaluate your example. Set solid biblical standards for yourself in what you read, listen to, and watch. Don't send mixed messages to your child.

▶ *Seek counseling if you are struggling with pornography issues.* Pornography destroys lives and relationships. Don't let this destructive problem linger like a snake ready to strike. Get help now for yourself and your family.

4. Getting Back on Track

If your child is struggling with pornography, here are some things you can do to help:

◆ **Don't ignore the issue.** Sometimes, even when they know their children are having a problem, parents struggle to confront it. Why? It could be they're struggling with the same or similar issues. Maybe they're hoping it's just something he will outgrow. But because of the destructive nature of this detour, you can't ignore it. Confront, discuss, and put a plan of action in order.

◆ **Reestablish boundaries.** Trust has been broken, so you need to pull the boundaries in a little closer. Depending on where your child was getting the pornography, you may need to place stronger restrictions on computer use, time with certain friends, cell phone use, and so forth. Make the boundaries clear, and hold your child accountable.

◆ **Discern the depth of the problem.** If you determine that your child's detour with pornography has moved into the area of addiction, this problem will probably be bigger than you can handle by yourself.

Consider contacting a local Christian counselor for help. Your pastor or student minister may be able to provide the names and contact information of reputable counselors.

- **Maintain an attitude of grace and forgiveness.** This doesn't mean you don't deal strongly with the problem. However, your child needs to recognize your continued love and support as you work to restore him and get him back on the right track.

1. Aaron Linne, "Picture Imperfect," *Living with Teenagers*, September 2009, 7.
2. Jason S. Carroll, et. al, "Generation XXX: Pornography Acceptance and Use Among Emerging Adults," *Journal of Adolescent Research*, Vol. 23, No. 1, 6-30 (2008).

PORNOGRAPHY

Purity Detour
HOMOSEXUALITY

1. Detour Description
Arguably, one of the biggest issues related to sexuality in today's culture is homosexuality. It is a firestorm of conflicting emotions, political ideologies, religious convictions, prejudices, and cultural norms. Given the culture in which today's children live, it's no wonder that many question their sexuality and/or experiment with same-gender sexual experiences. How you respond when you discover your child is wrestling with this issue is critical to helping him choose a lifestyle of purity. While these short paragraphs can't provide an exhaustive guide for dealing with this issue, the information that follows is meant to provide some basic facts and help as you walk through it with your child.

2. Reasons Your Child Might Take This Detour
- **Curiosity.** Many children, younger and older, are curious about sexual involvement with the same gender. They see it endorsed and supported in the media. Political campaigns can succeed or fail because of it. Religious leaders argue over it. Families split because of it. It is no wonder that children want to know what the big deal is.
- **Rapidly changing bodies and emotions.** The onset of adolescence brings an onslaught of rapid changes in one's body, mind, emotions, and social skills. As children begin to experience sexual feelings for the first time (or in stronger amounts), they don't know how to process those feelings and emotions. They are overwhelmed and want to find a way to channel this new aspect of their personhood. In some circumstances, children move toward homosexual activity.
- **Cultural endorsement.** Gay and lesbian relationships are the hallmark of popular television shows, movies, and even songs. It is difficult to find a television show or movie without a gay or lesbian

character being featured, usually in a positive light. Our culture, including the pop culture icons who flaunt their sexual orientation, creates conditions in which children accept the homosexuality of others as just another option and experiment with it themselves without any consideration of the consequences.

• **Personal experience.** Any number of significant experiences can influence a child's decision to act out or explore homosexual feelings. These experiences could include (but are not limited to) sexual abuse, harassment by peers, family dynamics and structure, and low self-worth. These factors are not necessarily determinants, but are rather influences in a person's framework from which choices are made.

3. Avoiding the Detour
• **What your child can do...**
  ▸ *Recognize that changes are normal.* A teenager caught in the tempest of rapidly changing hormones, emotions, and thoughts can begin to question those feelings and assume they are a marker of homosexuality. Teens must recognize that these conflicting emotions, thoughts, and feelings are natural. It is also important for teens not to act immediately on these feelings since they are not an accurate barometer of reality. In short, teens need to recognize that it's normal to feel a variety of emotions, but it's dangerous to act on them.
  ▸ *Learn to discern truth.* A part of becoming a mature adult is learning to discern the messages that are bombarding each of us every day. Teens (and adults) need to learn how to filter messages to determine what is truth and what is a carefully disguised lie—especially in the media. Because technology and media saturate the lives of teens (and adults), emerging generations must learn to think critically about media sources to determine the "spin" behind a message and to compare it with the unchanging truth in Scripture. This will help teens and young adults make wiser choices related to a life of purity.
  ▸ *Talk about feelings with parents and godly leaders.* Nothing causes a teen to lose his voice quite like talking about sexual issues. Teens get uncomfortable quickly when having an honest discussion about sex. Despite this discomfort, these conversations allow a teen to express both his emotions and questions, which are absolutely critical in helping him develop a lifestyle of purity.

HOMO-
SEXUALITY

♦ **What you can do...**

▸ *Talk about the issue.* Homosexuality is a common topic of discussion in culture. Make it a common topic of discussion in your home. If not, you will be abdicating your responsibility to inform your child about it. Use teachable moments—such as when a derogatory comment is made ("You're so gay") or a television program features an openly gay character—to talk about how a child or teen thinks or feels about this topic. These may not be the most comfortable conversations, but they are important nevertheless.

▸ *Create a healthy environment.* Your home and family should be a place in which your child develops healthy attitudes about sexuality and its related issues. From early on, communicate to your child the beauty and purpose of sexuality. Talk about God creating humanity as both male and female. Discuss the joy of sexual expression as a gift from God to be experienced in marriage. Discourage derogatory terminology regarding sex or sexual issues. Again as a parent, you set the stage for healthy sexual development.

▸ *Monitor your child's emotional attachments.* It is natural for a child or a teen to develop emotional attachments to other people. That is a measure of healthy emotional and social development. However, if your child becomes too attached to one person and cannot bear to be apart from that individual, this may be an indication of an unhealthy relationship. By initiating discussions and helping your child make wise choices, you create some control over a situation that could possibly create chaos.

4. Getting Back on Track

If your child is struggling with his or her sexuality, here are some things you can do to help:

♦ **Be careful about your initial response.** If you react too strongly or harshly when your child comes to you with questions, he may completely shut down and never approach you about this subject again. Don't act on your initial feelings (which is important for teens to learn as well). Just listen without judging and without drawing ill-formed conclusions.

♦ **Don't ignore your child's struggles, but don't focus solely on this issue.** Seek to strike a balance by discussing the issue with your child and thereby communicating that you are concerned about her.

At the same time, don't focus on this issue as the only thing that is important to you in her life. Talk about other stuff as well—friends, sports, current events, family struggles.

- **Demonstrate unconditional love.** If your child adopts an openly gay lifestyle, you may be tempted to lash out in anger, frustration, or revenge. You may want to withdraw your love and relationship in an attempt to control her. This approach does not achieve its desired effect. Mostly, it just drives your child deeper into the gay lifestyle. Moreover, such a conditional love does not mirror God's love toward us (John 3:16-17; Rom. 5:8).

- **Get professional help for you, your child, and your family.** It may be healthy for you to get counseling and guidance from a godly, trained therapist who has experience in helping families and parents deal with this issue. If your child is questioning his sexuality and is open to talking with a therapist, make every effort to make that happen.

HOMO-
SEXUALITY

Purity Detour
LIVING TOGETHER

1. Detour Description

More and more young couples move in together before they marry or in lieu of marriage altogether. While the reasons for this living arrangement vary, the consequences show the negative effects of such a lifestyle. For example, studies show that couples who lived together before marriage tend to divorce early in their marriage.[1] But statistics do not discuss the emotional consequences of giving your heart and body away to another person. Living together is a serious detour that can carry serious ramifications.

2. Reasons Couples Take This Detour

- **Trying it out.** Many couples choose to live together as a way to determine their compatibility as a married couple. But they fail to understand that living together and being married are two distinct experiences and come with different degrees of expectations and commitment. There are many downsides to "trying it out," but no real upside.
- **Convenience.** Many young adults see that living together is simply easier than living apart. Couples may claim that they are together all the time anyway and don't want the hassle of going home at night. Living together becomes an easy way around this. And it offers the couples every convenience of marriage, including sexual intimacy, while still providing "a way out" if the relationship hits a rocky or difficult phase.
- **Control.** One or both partners in a relationship may choose to live together in an effort to control the other person. This is a likely scenario when some sort of substance abuse is taking place or when there is an unhealthy balance in the relationship (co-dependence). A partner may see moving in as a way to monitor the other person's behavior or take care of the other person. But it really just builds on the already unhealthy nature of the relationship.

- **Finances.** Many couples choose to live together for financial reasons. Sharing space and living expenses, especially in today's uneven economy, is simply cheaper than going it alone. This often takes place in college and in the first years of a relationship when finances are stretched.
- **Culture.** The media today presents cohabitation as normal for a couple moving to the next stage of their relationship. This model of relationship can be seen in many major TV shows, movies, and book plots. It is seen as the next logical step before marriage. Choosing to stay celibate and foregoing this step in favor of marriage is seen as old-fashioned and archaic.

3. Avoiding the Detour

- **What your child can do...**
  - *Pay attention to cultural influences.* The influence of a godless world is often measured in tiny, subtle, insidious increments. Over time, a person can become desensitized to the influence of a godless culture and allow it to direct and influence one's behavior. As an adult, your child must take responsibility for the influences he is following and evaluate whether those cultural influences affirm or contradict biblical principles. Your child also needs to be alert to the temptation of sexual activity at this time since many couples who live together were sexually active before they started sharing a home.
  - *Maintain accountability.* By now, your child should have developed a network of relationships that provide accountability and support for a life of purity. She needs to lean on that accountability when tempted to forego the biblical structure for relationships.
  - *Develop a network of friends.* Sometimes people choose to move in with another person out of sheer loneliness. By developing friendships with a variety of people, your child can guard against loneliness that can lead to temptation. This also increases the possibility of accountability.
- **What you can do...**
  - *Set the example.* It's been noted already that the way you treat your spouse has a significant impact on how your child perceives the sanctity of marriage. If you do not treat your spouse with respect, love, and honor, your child may not see the necessity of such an institution. In fact, he may choose

LIVING TOGETHER

cohabitation directly because of what he sees lived out at home. Don't give your child any reason to forego healthy relationships because of your example.

▸ *Talk about the consequences of living together.* If your child asks your opinion about cohabitation, share honestly, but share in a spirit of love. Use this as an opportunity to talk about the negative consequences of choosing this living arrangement. Talk about the emotional, physical, and spiritual effects that she may face. Remind her of the different commitment levels that come with marriages and living together.

▸ *Help your child establish a solid financial foundation.* Use the childhood and teen years to teach concepts such as budgeting, saving, tithing, and balancing a checkbook. If an opportunity arises, talk about how much money your child will need to start out on his own. Begin to set aside funds for that time and challenge your child to contribute as well. This will help your child start strong and not be tempted to engage in cohabitation for financial reasons.

4. Getting Back on Track

If your child has already made the decision to live with a significant other, here are some things you can do to help:

• **Provide financial assistance when appropriate and possible.** While you want your child to develop financial independence, a little help in getting established can go a long way. If your child wants to move out of a cohabitation situation, offer to help with deposits. Go to consignment stores to look for furniture. Host a housewarming party. Do what you can to encourage independence.

• **State your case and then back off.** Chances are that your child knows that you disapprove of his decision to live with his girlfriend. It may be evident in your tone of voice or in the way you treat his significant other. If you feel the need to express your opinion, do so — once. And then back off. Do not constantly harp on the issue. This will not motivate your child to make any changes in his or her living situation. In many cases, such nagging just fuels the fire and drives your child deeper into the situation.

• **Continue to love unconditionally.** It may break your heart to see your child living with someone outside the covenant of marriage. You may be tempted to take out that heartbreak on your child by withdrawing your support and unconditional love from her, hoping that you can force a choice between you and a significant other. This is a dangerous move and could prove costly for you. In the end, it's nothing more than simple manipulation — and that is never a healthy foundation for a relationship or motivation for life change. Never base your love on whether or not you approve of your child's behavior. Again, God set the standard, loving us even when we did not deserve His love.

1. Sheri and Bob Stritof, "Cohabitation Facts and Statistics," About.com [online], cited 23 June 2010. Available from the Internet: *http://marriage.about.com/od/ cohabitation/qt/cohabfacts.htm*

LIVING
TOGETHER

FOR PURITY DETOURS

Paul told the Romans that everyone sins and falls short of God's glory (Rom. 3:23). On a very practical level, that means all of us will stray from His plan and His design at one time or another. Sometimes, that "straying" will involve losing our way on the path of purity. You may be looking for ways to prevent that from happening to your child, or your child may have wandered off the path already. In either case, here are some resources that will help you confront the detours and move back to a commitment to purity in every aspect of life.

- *When True Love Doesn't Wait* by D. Tony Rankin and Richard Ross (LifeWay Press, 1998): This booklet can help teenagers who are desperately seeking forgiveness in the area of purity.
- *Designed by God* by Pam Gibbs (LifeWay Press, 2004): This study is geared at helping students understand homosexuality from a biblical perspective.
- *Helping the Struggling Adolescent* by Dr. Les Parrott III (Zondervan, 2000): This practical resource is a tool and handbook for counselors, pastors, and youth workers and details over thirty common teenage problems arranged alphabetically. Includes such hot topics as anger, depression, drugs and alcohol, homosexuality, loneliness, masturbation, peer pressure, pornography, and shyness. Bound into the back of the book is a Counseling Guide that includes information on special issues in counseling and 43 Rapid Assessment Tests.

THE PARENT PARTNERSHIP

BY PAUL TURNER

Y ou must feel like you have waded through some pretty deep waters of parenting responsibilities coming through those first nine chapters. And quite honestly, it is a lot. But, one of the things you may have missed in your reading is that you do not have to go through it alone.

In fact, when it comes to parenting, thinking "I must do this alone" leads to a dead end physically, spiritually, and emotionally. It will cause you to wind up in a worn-out frenzy or throwing your hands in the air in disgust and possible defeat. No one wants to see that happen. I would much rather encourage you.

That's what this chapter is all about. It's designed to suggest some practical ways that your church can help you parent your children to love the Lord their God, with all their heart, soul and strength (Deut. 6—again).

For Starters

Of course, I understand that every church setting is different, just like every family is different. And that's OK. That's part of God's unique design for the body of Christ. But there are some universal things that need to be true before you can begin any kind of partnership with the leaders in your church—whether that be in children's ministry or student ministry. So, with that in mind, here are a few assumptions I am going to make about your church:

- **The leadership is concerned about parenting and families.** I am assuming that you are part of a church body where the spiritual leaders have a heart for families and are committed to doing everything they can to equip you for your task.

- **The leadership of your church is making the most of the resources available to equip you to be a Christ-honoring parent.** It's one thing to say you have a heart for families, but church leaders need to move to the next level and put those words into action. There are numerous ways they can express their willingness to help you, and they won't be perfect all the time. But they need to avoid providing only lip service to this vital area of ministry.

- **Your church's leaders may not have a comprehensive strategy in place right now, but they are willing to invest time and resources into thinking holistically about presenting a comprehensive parenting strategy that includes parents of babies, preschoolers, children, youth, and young adults.** A lot of churches are just now picking up on the importance of equipping parents to embrace their role as spiritual developers in the home. Your church may be in that boat. Your leaders may have come to the game late, but they are coming ready to play.

On the Same Page

As I mentioned earlier, healthy churches have an effective strategy for resourcing parents as the primary developer of their students. While your church may not have everything you need to be a successful parent, it can provide vital information, resources, events, and other tools to help you along the way.

Just as there is no such thing as a perfect parent (or a perfect church, for that matter), there is no single, perfect way to get at this whole responsibility of ministering to families. But I do want to share a possible way for your church to help parents become effective developers of their children, while taking into account its own unique culture when it comes to creating programs and establishing long-range plans.

Your church may have younger youth ministers who don't have a lot of parenting experience of their own. This is often the case with student ministers, who love teenagers, but don't have teens in their own home. It could also be true with a young children's minister who is single or who hasn't started a family yet. It would be easy to wonder about how ministers in these situations can possibly offer anything to a discussion on parenting, but don't automatically discount this individual's potential as a beneficial resource. This minister may be able to provide insight from past ministerial experience or can support programs that encourage you as a parent.

You also may find that there are other parents in your church who have already navigated the waters of parenting in a particular life stage — or are navigating the waters with you. These fellow travellers can be a good resource for you, as well. You can learn from one another and provide a level of accountability for one another.

In some situations, it might be that you are actually the best person to move into a leadership position. You can establish a solid relationship with the staff member responsible for your area of concern and work with him to identify ways your church can reach out to parents and equip them to raise their children in a biblical way. I know the very thought might leave you saying "Yikes!" right now, but it might be easier to do than you are thinking and feeling at this moment. And don't forget, if God is truly leading you in this direction, He will give you the tools you need to make it a reality. He will not give you a job and leave you floundering in your own strength.

Your church may have a seasoned leader who is committed to helping parents accept the role as the primary developer of their children. If so, count it all joy. But if you find yourself in a church that may not have a strong desire to help parents, do not jump ship. Sometimes church leaders have great intentions and little (or no) understanding of how to pull a program for parents off. If you find yourself in that place, here are some tips to help you intentionally work with your church's leadership to create a support system for parents who are trying to lead their children toward spiritual maturity and a lifetime commitment to the path of purity.

Commit to a Biblical Model

So what does a biblical model look like? In chapter 4, you read about Deuteronomy 6 and the important role parents play in teaching their children to love the Lord their God, with all their heart, soul, and strength. If your church is committed to supporting the home, then this passage is foundational.

Churches and children's or student ministries who love you, your child, and God's Word will be intentional about helping and resourcing you. But you also have a responsibility. Too many families are intentional about teaching their children to capture everything the prevailing culture has to offer, even if it means losing their souls in the process (Mark 8:36).

That may sound harsh, but it's true. I've said throughout this chapter that parents are the primary spiritual developers of their children, which means they are *always* teaching. The only question is, *What is being taught?* If parents aren't intentional about helping their children learn to love God with their entire beings, they are teaching them—whether they recognize it or not—that the most important things in life have nothing to do with God. He sits somewhere further down on the list of priorities, something that can be tended to on Sundays and during any "spare time" along the way.

At the same time, church leaders need to remember that many families have moved beyond the days of "Leave it to Beaver" homes. These days, they might look more like the blended family of "Yours, Mine, and Ours." But the changing make-up of the family in our culture does not negate the responsibility of parents to pursue a biblical model and to take their role seriously as primary spiritual developer.

While it may be more difficult to reach out to families where children spend some time at one house and some time at another, it is important that parents and churches find a way to work together to promote true spiritual development in the lives of children and teenagers. Parents need church leaders who will encourage the biblical model found in Deuteronomy 6. And those leaders need to commit themselves to providing resources and support for every kind of family God brings into their sphere of influence.

Failing to recognize (or adapt to) the changing nature of the family isn't an option. Neither is refusing to develop creative ways to communicate the unchanging truth of the gospel. Christian parents need to work hard at doing what God has called them to do. Churches need to support that effort by embracing the truth and presenting it in many ways across a broad church landscape.

Move Ahead

We'd like to think that any partnership between the church and families would flow smoothly. We'd like to believe that such an ideal relationship would come complete with heavenly choirs, soft light, and some kind of divine message that provides all the answers. We'd love to see a wide-open door that leads down the path of purity.

Unfortunately, it doesn't always work that way. If parents and leaders in your church have never really tried to create a partnership, the initial stages can be bumpy. The time it takes to launch the partnership can raise unexpected questions and snags as parents and leaders learn how to work together and support one another. But even though the going might be rough at first, it's definitely worth the effort. Both sides just have to be willing to show patience and grace.

Parents and church leaders can start by allowing each other to be who they are and to start where they are. That sounds sort of weird, but in my experience of working with families, expectations can create the first casualties in any kind of partnership. Individuals get locked down because they don't feel like they can live up to the standard placed in front of them. And while it's healthy to understand limitations (since God's strength is made perfect in our weakness, 2 Cor. 12:9), it's hard to avoid the temptation to wallow in a false sense of inadequacy.

Whether you're a parent or a leader, the next time you feel overwhelmed by the expectations of the partnership, take a look at Luke 2. Go ahead and do it right now. Take out your Bible—or your phone or laptop—and start reading at verse 41 or so. Work your way through the end of the chapter.

Read it slowly and put yourself in the place of Mary and Joseph. They were parenting the Son of God—which was a pretty big task if you ask me. But they lost Him. They lost the Son of God!

If you think you have issues as a parent or in ministering to parents, think how you would feel with that kind of pressure on you. In today's culture, an Amber Alert would go out for Jesus, and Mary and Joseph would be questioned. People would be saying all kinds of things about their lack of parenting skills. They would feel overwhelmed as parents, and it would be a tough case study for any church minister to give them any kind of comfort or advice.

After three days, Mary and Joseph found Jesus in the temple in Jerusalem, but they had been worried sick. Mary asked Jesus, "Son, why have You treated us like this? Your father and I have been anxiously searching for You" (v. 48). That's a typical parental response. She did not look at Him and make sure He was OK. Instead, she essentially asked Him, "What were you thinking?!"

Mary and Joseph were real-life parents. They got some things right, but they also tripped up on some other things. In other words, they were normal human beings.

But one thing they got right was the whole Deuteronomy 6 passage. We know that because when Jesus was an adult, some religious leaders quizzed Him about the greatest commandment (Mark 12:28-30). In response, He reminded them of the *Shemah* (Deut. 6:4-9). I'm convinced that Jesus learned that from His earthly parents. They taught Him, the human side of Him, to "love the LORD your God with all your heart, with all your soul, and with all your strength." Luke even hints at that in the last verse of chapter 2, where he said that Jesus submitted to His parents and grew in wisdom, stature, favor with God, and favor with others (Luke 2:51-52).

If you and your church leaders are getting a late start on all of this, do not worry. Start where you are. Work with your staff to find some parents in your church who have been intentional in parenting. Ask them to be mentors in the area of parenting. They can provide wise counsel for church programming and encouragement for parents who are going through difficult times.

As you look at where your church stands in relationship to the parent partnership, you might feel a little guilty. But you need to remember that guilt is not of God. Whether you're a parent or a leader, confess any known sin and move on. Do not let yourself be mired down. Keep moving forward.

Practical Ideas for the Partnership

If you're not sure where to start, here are a few ideas to get your ministry moving. These can become the basis for any expectations related to a parent partnership.

- Enlist a group of parents to go through *Indelible Parenting* (LifeWay Press, 2008), a four-unit Bible study based on Deuteronomy 6.
- Lead parents to use *30 Days* (LifeWay Press, 2003), a month-long resource that connects parents with their students.
- Use the free twice-a-week family devotions called *Heart Connex*. You can have these delivered to you by signing up at *www.heartconnex.com*.
- Use *Living with Teenagers* magazine for monthly support and informative articles. Go to *www.lifeway.com/livingwithteenagers* for more information.
- Visit each parent and explain the idea of a parent partnership and the opportunities and resources described in this chapter.
- At least twice a year, offer parents a chance to be involved in the partnership.
- Make use of some free articles and other parenting resources found at *www.lifeway.com/students*.
- Make sure any resources used are based on Scripture and contribute to the goal of developing students, including the biblical importance of living out a commitment to purity.

General Resources for Parents

As you've worked through this book, you've probably noticed the lists of resources at the end of some of the chapters. We hope you find these helpful as you walk the path of purity with your family. Here are some additional resources that specifically address your task as a parent.

- *Living with Teenagers* magazine: This monthly magazine equips parents to raise teens who know God, own their faith, and make their faith known.
- *Indelible Parenting* by Bob Bunn (LifeWay Press, 2008): This study leads parents through the biblical principles of spiritual leadership found in Deuteronomy 6.
- *Pure Parenting* by Lynn Pryor and Deanna Harrison (LifeWay Press, 2009): This is a practical guide to equip parents to raise children who embrace the pledge behind True Love Waits to live a life of purity.
- *Student Ministry and the Supremacy of Christ* by Richard Ross (CrossBooks Publishing, 2009)
- *HomeLife* magazine: This monthly magazine provides tools that equip families to experience dynamic, healthy, Christ-centered living.
- *Are You Developing Students or Your Student Ministry?* by Jeff Pratt and Scott Stevens (LifeWay Press, 2010): This book explains LifeWay's strategy for students' spiritual development—KNOWN—to student ministers and volunteer workers.
- *Engaging Your Teen's World: Become a Culturally Savvy Parent* by Brian Housman (Brazos Press, 2009): Parents are encouraged in this book to move past unhealthy "us vs. them" mentalities and lead their teen to redeem the culture instead. This conversational book guides parents to become a greater influence in their teen's world without squelching their child's individuality.
- *Wild Things: The Art of Nurturing Boys* by Stephen James and David Thomas (Tyndale House, 2009): This engaging owner's manual on boys aged 2 to 22 provides real-life examples to illustrate characteristics frequently shared among boys of similar ages and provide guidance on what boys need most during those stages.
- *Raising Girls* by Melissa Trevathan and Sissy Goff (Zondervan, 2007): Journey into the heart of girls in this book to help you understand your daughter's different stages of development: what is normal, what is not, and how to relate effectively.

Concluding THOUGHTS

As you've worked your way through the pages of this book, you have literally covered a lifetime of parenting. From birth to adulthood, you've walked through the joys of significant markers that shape individuals and families. You've also been introduced to the way those markers influence your child's walk down the path of purity.

It's our desire that the words you've read have challenged you and encouraged you. We hope that we've helped you see purity in a way you may have never seen it before. We wanted to drive home the truth that this is a process, rather than a one-time talk or ceremony. We also wanted to share our belief that you are the primary influence on how this process works itself out through your child's experiences.

You've probably picked up on some recurring themes along the way as well. Since each of these chapters (and even the content related to markers within chapters) was written independently, none of that was planned. And we weren't trying to be repetitive. It's just that some very important truths always seem to rise to the top when it comes to parenting and purity.

- **God has a plan.** He has a plan for purity—sex is a great thing, but it's reserved for the context of a marriage relationship. But He also has a plan for you and for your child (Jer. 1:5; 29:11). He placed you and your children together because He knew you needed each other and that they could never successfully walk the path of purity alone.
- **Temptation is out there.** Since God created sexuality as a blessing, we can be sure that Satan is working overtime to pervert God's plan. He will do everything he can to make sin look enticing and to convince us that there is a better way. He's been doing it since the garden of Eden: "Did God really say...?" (Gen. 3:1). He's still at it today.
- **Planning ahead and setting proper boundaries are important.** Your teen can't just attack this sexual monster on her own. You have to work

together to understand the dangers and the most effective strategies. And you have to set boundaries that will make the best use of those strategies. When a boundary is crossed (and they will be), there has to be a consequence. But there also has to be an encouragement to return to the authority of the boundary from that point forward.

- **Communication is vital.** Whether it's teaching your child the proper names for body parts, initiating ongoing discussions about God's plan for sex, or talking with your young adult about the dangers of homosexuality or living together, communication can't be overrated. Creating a culture of communication means talking and listening. It also means you are not afraid to tackle tough subjects in an honest and loving way.
- **Without support and accountability, the path of purity becomes a lonely, dangerous place.** Making a commitment to purity is incredibly important, but it's just the beginning. Your child will need you to walk with him at every marker. He will need your encouragement. He will need you to show him how to choose friends and identify significant adults who can provide additional guidance when you're not around. And, if a detour occurs, he will need you to love him, even when you've been hurt yourself.

We affirm that you really are the primary spiritual developer of your children, and hopefully we have better equipped you to carry out this role. We trust that this book has encouraged you to grab that mantle and embrace the calling God has placed on your life.

God bless you and your family as you make your way down the path of purity.

Two Ways to Earn Credit
for Studying LifeWay Christian Resources Material

CHRISTIAN GROWTH STUDY PLAN

CONTACT INFORMATION:
Christian Growth Study Plan
One LifeWay Plaza, MSN 117
Nashville, TN 37234
CGSP info line 1-800-968-5519
www.lifeway.com/CGSP
To order resources 1-800-485-2772

Christian Growth Study Plan resources are available for course credit for personal growth and church leadership training.

Courses are designed as plans for personal spiritual growth and for training current and future church leaders. To receive credit, complete the book, material, or activity. Respond to the learning activities or attend group sessions, when applicable, and show your work to your pastor, staff member, or church leader. Then go to *www.lifeway.com/CGSP*, or call the toll-free number for instructions for receiving credit and your certificate of completion.

For information about studies in the Christian Growth Study Plan, refer to the current catalog online at the CGSP Web address. This program and certificate are free LifeWay services to you.

Need a CEU?

CONTACT INFORMATION:
CEU Coordinator
One LifeWay Plaza, MSN 150
Nashville, TN 37234
Info line 1-800-968-5519
www.lifeway.com/CEU

Receive Continuing Education Units (CEUs) when you complete group Bible studies by your favorite LifeWay authors.

Some studies are approved by the Association of Christian Schools International (ACSI) for CEU credits. Do you need to renew your Christian school teaching certificate? Gather a group of teachers or neighbors and complete one of the approved studies. Then go to *www.lifeway.com/CEU* to submit a request form or to find a list of ACSI-approved LifeWay studies and conferences. Book studies must be completed in a group setting. Online courses approved for ACSI credit are also noted on the course list. The administrative cost of each CEU certificate is only $10 per course.